# Show Some Respect!

## The Sound and the Fury of Junior Football

### By Chris Kirkham

**PURE PHASE PUBLISHING**

First Published by Pure Phase Publishing
88 Manor Road, Derby, DE72 3LN
www.purephase-publishing.co.uk

Part of The People's History of Football series
www.peopleshistoryoffootball.com

ISBN  978-0-9561144-7-1

## About the author

Christopher William Kirkham was born in Bridlington, East Yorkshire in 1971 and was educated at Martongate Primary school before moving onto Headlands School in Bridlington. He worked within retail for ten years before searching for a career in football coaching.

After successfully completing many courses with national governing bodies and East Riding College, he took up voluntary coaching roles in the area including at Hull City. He then ventured to America, where his coaching story really begins. He had considerable success with girls' football (soccer) during this time and spent 5 years working alongside coaches from all over the UK and USA. His experiences abroad were to lead him to opportunities in the UK where he coached and worked at Manchester United Soccer Schools, Bobby Charlton Soccer Schools, Scarborough School of Excellence, Everton Football Club and Sheffield Wednesday Football Club. He also liaised with Sunderland, Newcastle, Manchester United and Liverpool football clubs, organising trips for local players to attend games and to visit stadiums.

From 2001 he began his own coaching schools and built up a creditable reputation featuring in the local newspaper most weeks with his contributions to local football. A holiday soccer school was created and in 2006 came the birth of a new football club, The Burlington Jackdaws.

As well as being a coach, he is an avid Manchester United fan and goes to Old Trafford whenever he can. He is also a supporter of the England national team and visited Japan in 2002 for the World Cup.

He found time to qualify in other sports and his full-time job, (on top of coaching and writing) led him to Physical Education positions in secondary schools in Hull, Scarborough and Bridlington. He has had long and short term contracts and currently works at

Archbishop Sentamu Academy in Hull and is a scout for Hull City F.C. In 2010-11 he sent three young players to Hull with great success as all three were signed by the Tigers.

He has also set up after school clubs in his home town of Bridlington where he has lived all his life, excluding the time in America. Mum, Marian, helps The Jackdaws on the fundraising side as well as being the club treasurer. Dad, Dave, is a Director of a large firm in Bridlington where brother Ben also works.

Chris has a partner in Justine and three beautiful step-daughters, who he is extremely proud to have brought up over the last decade. Lily Mae 10, plays football, is an avid Manchester United fan and goes to games with Chris. Lily plays in a boys team and has also excelled in girls football at Centre of Excellences. Bronte, the middle one, is now a keen footballer. Having traipsed round many football matches with Lily and Chris, she decided to go for it herself! At 12, Bronte enjoys the game and is a keen learner at school. The eldest of the bunch is Shanie who has no interest in football at all, except for player's legs! Now 18, Shanie has a part time job, has just completed a college course and hopes to one day work abroad.

Justine has realised over the years that only one thing matters in her household and that is football; as she trips over the large collection of memorabilia, trophies, awards and of course footballs. She works part time and spends the remaining hours cleaning up after the family! A caring mother, Justine spends many a blustery morning on touchlines and is often a football widow.

The Burlington Jackdaws have been recognised locally and were nominated for the East Riding Club of the Year in 2008 and 2011 and the FA Charter Standard Club of the Year 2011.

# Acknowledgements

The idea and concept of this book is to continue improving standards on our touchlines and pitches at junior football and tell the story of the Respect campaign with all its great ambassadors. The hope is that clubs will supply a copy to each and every parent to help them realise the damage that can be caused.

My aim is that the book reaches every junior football household and watching families. The back cover if bought into by clubs can be used for sponsors effectively costing the club nothing whilst the sponsors advert will go out to every member in the club.

The question is: how did the game come to this? as I sit writing with a stiff neck through stress and lack of sleep from a most bewildering situation. What do they want? and can the junior clubs, FA and beyond give them the answers as they chase their child's dream? Or is it the players or coaches fault?

I began writing this in November 2010, and haven't stopped since.

I would like to thank all those for their input and interest in the publication and friends and family for their support over the time of writing and those throughout my coaching career. Most particularly: Tony McCormick, Jay Cochrane, Barry Scott, John Gibson MBE and Cyril Skinner along with all at the Bridlington Free Press and Bobby Charlton Soccer Schools who continue to support him.

Thanks go to my Mum and Dad who spent many parents' evenings at school, with teachers complaining that all I wrote about was football. I'm still reminded of the story of when I wrote that if I was on the moon, I would start my own football team! I'd like to praise my partner Justine who has listened to every click of the keyboard and listened to the stories time and time again. Along with my travelling work companion the Brazilian Marcos Brown-Garcia who has heard the full assignment. Finally for Dave Fisher for proof reading it and my brother Ben, for scanning the stories.

Without the help of Stewart Smith, the publisher, and the magazine When Saturday Comes, who without it, I would never have seen Stewart's advert and hit the mouse button in contacting him.

The research has led me to liaising with the FA, and several county FAs and leagues. To all those I've "bugged" a big "cheers" from me and hope I this helps your causes. The input from Mal Lee at the Don't X The Line campaign (the man behind the initial set up of the Respect campaign and the barriers), has been so valuable along with the support from Paul Cooper at Give Us Back Our Game. Dermot Collins, the FA Respect manager, has respected all my e-mails and his points are the highlight of the story.

Finally the other contributors of the book are all mentioned as you read on, and I couldn't have done it all without all the stories. If you are one of those perpetrators who have read about yourself, then I thank you again for providing the tales and hope you learn from your mistakes and take your clubs forward.

Some will sneer, some will jeer and some will choose to ignore it. It is maybe those people that I and all of these people above are trying to reach.

This book is in no way affiliated to the FA and was not meant to upset anybody or be a threat. It is simply to help; and with your support, I believe it can help the way of the touchlines, pitches and problems out there.

The views are my views only (along with those that have been written on forums or contributed) and not intended to be representative of every club, league and FA. There is a cross section of stories, and I have not set out to trip anybody up. This was also not meant to put any body off joining a junior club and is intended to give us all a platform to succeed, as some chase their boy's and girl's hopes and dreams and put REPECT back onto the sidelines for good.

The writing of this book is how I felt at the time. Much like the writing of a song. My overall view is that this is just a minority, like anything in life that hampers other people's progress. The stories are told as if I was chatting to you over a pint down the pub.
It was written to help the campaign and has received support from all quarters involved.

This book is dedicated to the memory of my Grandad and friend Patrick Butler.

The Premier League launched a 'RESPECT' campaign in 2008 to stop verbal abuse on officials.

Who is to blame?

You decide…

"The negative side of football. The negative side of our society. People sometimes go to football and bring to it the negative aspects of our society."

Jose Mourinho

# Contents

**Part Four**

- Respect United
- Zero Tolerance ( Sale United )
- Don't X The Line
- Keep it Shut Survey
- Codes of Conduct

**Part Five**

- My Story ( Reprise III)
- The Solutions
- The Positives
- The Results
- The Conclusion

**Sources**

**Thanks**

# Foreword

With the book only hours away from the printers, England was thrown into turmoil as riots broke out across the country. What shocked the nation was the lack of morality shown by the rioters, most of whom were simply looters, opportunistically stealing whatever they could lay their hands on. Innocent by-standers were attacked and mugged; cars, homes and businesses were set ablaze.

The riots had been blamed on disenfranchised youth; but when the identity of the first looters was revealed, the group included a teaching assistant, a millionaire's daughter and many others in gainful employment who had all cast aside basic values of decency, honesty and respect to contribute to the misery of thousands of others.

The riots followed shortly after the phone-hacking scandal in Britain which also called into question standards of the countries morality. This time the culprits were highly paid journalists, private investigators and police officers, who had all played their part in a scandal that appalled the public and led to the closure of the News of the World, one of the world's oldest newspapers.

When we also consider the recent MPs expenses scandal, which saw MPs being imprisoned for dishonesty, we can clearly see that a lack of basic values can be found across the full spectrum of British society.

Against this backdrop, is it any wonder that we see a lack of respect in football from players and spectators alike? After all, football does not stand outside of society.

The difference is that football is trying to do something about it. Step-by-step, changes are being made to make the football world a nicer place. In fact, these changes have been happening for a few years thanks to a few committed individuals.

Chris Kirkham is one of these people. After observing what was happening at youth level in the game, Chris was determined to drive change and set up his own club, the Burlington Jackdaws based in Bridlington.

With continual reference to the FAs official Respect campaign, Chris incorporated a number of elements into the structure of his club to benefit the most important people – the children playing the game. Qualified coaches, codes of conduct, caring about the development of players and not just results… all these things make a difference and make our parks a more pleasant place on a Sunday morning.

In a country labelled as a "broken society" by the ruling Prime Minister, football is an area that can help to introduce basic standards of respect and discipline into a young person's life. Football has and always will be a popular game amongst the inner cities where many of the recent riots took place. Maybe football can contribute, in some small way, to a better future? Football may only be a small part of society but engages with thousands of children every week.

Stories such as Chris' provide hope for the future of football and show the way forward. Read on and hopefully you will be inspired to make your own small change.


Stewart Smith – author and publisher
(published as *Edgar Smith*)

"If the enjoyment is taken away by Adults who rant and rave on the touchline and the grassroots game becomes in effect a computer game controlled by dads , the opportunity for young players to plant the seeds of a lifelong love affair with the game will be dismissed."

*Les Howie*
*Head of Grassroots Football for the FA*

## Introduction

In August 2008 The FA Respect campaign was launched with the expectation that by the Season 2010/2011, all junior football teams would have safety barriers around their pitches for spectators, parents, grandparents, friends, cats, dogs and whoever shows up on the day to stand behind and support their child from. The campaign also covered the Premier League as well as the rest of senior football. Respect for referees was high on the agenda after a series of incidents had been highlighted in the media.

This book focuses on the reason for the barriers in junior football. Why they have to be there, and why they have to work. The Respect Zone barriers had been tested extensively for durability, safety, convenience and effectiveness. It was hoped the barriers would be the answer to some of the problems junior football had been facing. I wrote this because I hoped it would reach each junior footballing household. My intention was not to put people off, but to warn them of the pitfalls and give readers an idea of how not to behave, along with making it clear it is only a minority who tarnish the games reputation.

The safety of players and spectators is of paramount importance and the Respect Zone barrier system ensures that a safe, effective, designated spectator area is created quickly and easily. This is all good and well, as long as the parents respect the Respect Zone. The barriers are easy to assemble and have become part of the match day preparation.

I have trawled through many websites, forums and blogs in my research; as well as listening to many a radio phone-in and reading magazines. I found a lot of horrific stories from the front line and share these with you over the following pages.

One of the most remarkable stories I came across was reported by the Liverpool Echo in 2010, two years after the launch of the Respect Campaign. During an Under 15 football match, young players were left injured and shaken after an incident that shook junior football.

### An FA Respect campaign pole was used against the kids as a weapon!

The FA Respect campaign promotes fair play and equality, yet a Saturday morning clash in Liverpool erupted into a mass brawl in the 70th minute, which led to the match being abandoned. In total nine players were sent off during the match following the incident.

In what had previously been a competitive, yet fairly contested game, it is alleged that several players reacted with their fists after an incident on the pitch. Players from both sides became involved in a punch-up, before an unnamed player allegedly came on to the pitch wielding the Respect pole. A number of players were struck by the weapon, causing cuts and bruises.

The coach said: "In the 30 years I have been involved in football I have never seen anything like it. To use a weapon on a football field is totally out of order, and for that weapon to be an FA Respect campaign pole is quite ironic. There is no place in football for that kind of behaviour". The match referee submitted his post match report to the FA and the incident was investigated.

It is hoped every parent, player, coach, official and onlooker at every junior football club in the country, will get the chance to read this book and whether I alter things or not, I will feel I have contributed to helping address a problem that has been killing our kids game. Some people blame the external pressures of modern culture such as the media; others blame referees. However, for the parents, the real answer is often staring at them in the mirror every day.

Many parents are brilliant and do a splendid job every time they watch their child play. I encourage those parents to read on, as those people can hopefully help me, the FA and Respect United fulfil our dreams of being able to watch our children play football in a friendly, unthreatening, safe and best of all, a fun environment.

Read this book in sections on your break, or over the course of a season. Give the views and stories some thought and think of how you would tackle that situation?

Most of all, as a parent, possibly of an Under 7 player just about to join a club, please don't be put off in any way from signing up your child. Remember that the unfortunate incidents detailed in this book represent just a minority that occasionally spoil the fun for others, as matches are played up and down the country every weekend.

A local Football Association, the North Riding County FA, introduced the Respect Zone barriers early and Jamie Clarke, Respect Lead Officer wrote on the NRFA website that there had been positive signs already.

The Respect Zone barrier now is an essential part of any match day, from preparing the goals to removing the dog dirt (nice!) - The barriers must now go up!

Enjoy the book, enjoy the stories and most of all, please help to make a change.

I've chosen some songs along the way to accompany each section, some I like some I don't really care for, but all are relevant to the campaign.

# Welcome to Respect

The following extracts are taken from the North Riding FA website. You may wish to read through the FA guidance, or refer back to it as you progress through the book.

Respect is The FA's programme of activities to combat unacceptable behaviour in our game at every level - on the pitch and from the sidelines. Respect is a key programme for the FA and contributes towards Goal 2 (Raising Standards) within the FA National Game Strategy. The National Game Strategy involved the single biggest review ever undertaken of grassroots football involving 16,000 stakeholders from all aspects of the game. This was followed up in North Riding CFA through online questionnaires and interactive consultation workshops and the top priority both nationally and locally is to tackle abusive touchline behaviour and abuse towards referees.

The North Riding County FA will support Clubs to integrate the four key messages of the Respect Programme. These are:

Step 1: Codes of conduct for players, referees, coaches and spectators which sets down basic principles that everyone must sign and adhere to.

Step 2: Designated Spectators' Areas defined by touchline barriers to keep spectators back from the pitch.

Step 3: Captains taking responsibility for their players and becoming the main point of contact for the referee.

Step 4: Referees managing the game and dealing with any open show of dissent

## Frequently Asked Questions

To help you, we have placed a series of Frequently Asked Questions Below:

### What is the Respect programme?

- Respect is a cross-game programme dedicated to improving standards of behaviour at all levels of football

- The programme will be implemented in professional and grassroots football, and encompasses not only respect towards match officials, but also the conduct of overly-competitive coaches and parents on the sidelines at grassroots youth games.

- It represents a shared commitment between The FA, Premier League, Football League, PFA, LMA, referees, County FAs and regional and local leagues.

- Ultimately Respect is about creating positive football environments, making poor and abusive behaviour unacceptable in football, and retaining more referees.

### Why it is being introduced?

- The message that behaviour is the No.1 concern in the grassroots game came through loud and clear in the massive research campaign The FA undertook before publishing its National Game Strategy earlier this year.

- The research compiled the views of over 37,000 participants, including players, coaches, referees, volunteers and fans. The feedback confirmed that parental pressure is one of the main reasons why young players drop out of the game, while poor behaviour by coaches, players and parents towards referees sees around 7,000 referees quit the game every year.

**OK fine, but how do you know the Respect programme is going to work when it is rolled out?**

- During the second half of last season, The FA conducted a week 10-week pilot scheme in 15 adult and youth leagues across the country, which was monitored on a weekly basis.

- The pilot comprised a combination of three measures: allowing only the captain to speak to the referee, erecting barriers along the touchlines to keep spectators back, and codes of conduct with related sanctions for everyone involved in the participating clubs. Over 300 teams, 166 referees and 4,500 players were involved.

- The overwhelming positive feedback from referees, players, coaches and parents, revealed that the measures had a tangible impact on behaviour on the pitch and sidelines, and informed The FA's plans for the 2008-09 season

- Full details of the pilot will be released ahead of the grassroots launch for Respect

**How have players, clubs, managers, etc. been informed about the new measures?**

- There have been meetings held with leagues, clubs, managers, referees at the Professional Game level, and meetings with County FAs at National Game Level. Guidance notes have also been distributed to specific groups.

- FA Chief Executive Brian Barwick is also writing to 1,300 leagues asking them to join Respect.

- We are also making a "toolkit" available to leagues, clubs, captains, referees and County FAs

- There is a real support across the game for what we are trying to achieve with Respect.

- There is also downloadable information on TheFA.com/Respect.

**Why is Respect starting at the bottom rather than the top of the game?**

- It was important to test the measures in a properly conducted pilot scheme, which realistically can only be done at grassroots level.

- It was always the intention to engage the professional game for 2008-09 and we now have a whole-game approach, which has been largely guided by the results of the pilot.

- We are also responding to a clear message from the grassroots (which represents the overwhelming bulk of the game) to tackle behaviour.

- In our consultation for The FA National Game Strategy, the behaviour of pushy parents and coaches on the sidelines, and the abuse of referees, were highlighted as the biggest concerns (80% and 73% respectively as their No.1 concern).

**Have sanctions for dissent been increased under The FA's disciplinary system?**

- No. We are confident that the combination of the new measures and the existing sanctions will be effective in tackling dissent and confrontational behaviour.

**So how much is it costing?**

- The FA is contributing £1m to providing support materials, training, monitoring, awareness and PR campaigns.

- However, much of the delivery is through existing staff and resources. This is a real priority and something we are committed to doing properly.

- The Football Foundation has also committed £1m towards the cost of the spectator barriers.

## So how will Respect work in the Professional Game?

- The Football Association, Premier League, Football League, Professional Footballers' Association (PFA), League Managers Association (LMA) and Professional Game Match Officials (PGMO) are working in partnership in the professional game, with the emphasis on the relationship between referees, and players and managers.

- The key steps being introduced to the Premier League and Football League are:

    1. Referee managing the game / captain's taking responsibility for the conduct of their team.
    2. Pre-match briefing meeting with referee and managers/captains.
    3. Team handshake before kick-off.
    4. Behaviour in the technical area.

- The Respect programme in the professional game will be seen for the first time on the weekend of 9/10 August, including The FA Community Shield between Manchester United and Portsmouth on Sunday 10 August.

## Why has the "captains-only" message been watered down?

- It has been adapted, rather than watered down. While the captain's only measure reduced dissent, many referees in the pilot felt it restricted their ability to man-manage and interact with the players.

- In addition, many captains and their team-mates didn't fully understand the system and wanted to be able to communicate with the match officials.

- The Respect programme is now concentrating on the key problem areas of harassment and challenging and asking captains to take a more proactive role

- This approach, which will help rather than hinder interaction between referees and captains, will be standard across all levels of the game.

## Do you really think this will change behaviour in the professional game?

- There is a general agreement that these measures will improve the relationship between match officials and players and coaches and improve behaviour as a result.

- Everyone has bought into this, including the PFA and the LMA

- Referees are also being instructed to take a firm line on applying the Laws of the Game, especially in the areas of dissent and abusive behaviour.

- There will always be controversial incidents but we are aiming for long-term improvement.

## And how will Respect work in the grassroots game?

The programme at a local level will focus on four practical steps to improve behaviour, both on the pitch and on the sidelines:

1. Codes of Conduct

2. Designated Spectators' Areas

3. Captain taking responsibility

4. Referee managing the game

## I play in a local FA registered league - how can my team sign up for Respect?

- The FA is making Respect available to all grassroots leagues, with an easy-to-use "toolkit" comprising guidance notes, codes of conduct, Captain's guidance leaflets and Respect armbands, and advice on purchasing the barriers.

- County FA Referee Development Officers and Welfare Officers will help with the Respect implementation and offer guidance and support to referees, leagues and clubs

- We want to see Respect in operation around the country and we are working with the County FAs to involve as many leagues as possible

- We are now in the process of inviting leagues to get involved in Respect, but we won't have the final numbers until the end of August/start of September

- The initial response has been very positive: there is a general understanding of the benefits involved in being part of Respect

## Is Respect obligatory at grassroots level?

- It will be mandatory in Charter Standard Leagues only (49 taking part in the pilot).

- We hope that the accessible nature of the programme will encourage clubs and leagues to get involved, and to this point The FA is working with all the County FAs to maximise participation.

- This is a long-term programme and we will look at the impact of the 2008-09 measures before deciding how to take it forward for the following season.

- We are looking into how it could become mandatory for 2009-10.

## How can referees get involved?

- Referees operating in the leagues that have adopted Respect can receive special training from the County Referee Development Officers on the new measures.

- This is in addition to the on-going mentoring and support network. We have also produced a guide for referees explaining the new measures. The programme will be embedded in future referee training.

- Referees wishing to get involved in a "Respect league" should contact their local RDO.

**Why don't you make the Respect measures obligatory?**

- This is a long-term approach, and we are going step-by-step

- The response from County FAs, leagues and individual clubs has been outstanding so far

- There may well be mandatory aspects to Respect further down the line, but first we will assess the impact of this coming season

**What are the penalties for breaching the codes of conduct?**

- The codes of conduct also carry related actions

- There can be action from the relevant County FA and/or The FA. We are trying to instill respect as a general climate in which people can enjoy the game.

**How does Respect link into The FA National Game Strategy?**

- The issue of Respect and improving behaviour is a central theme of the NGS.

- It also links in with some of The Football Association's other priorities, such as boosting participation, raising standards, developing better players, and increasing referee recruitment and retention.

- We are trying to improve the general culture of the game to make it more accessible and enjoyable for everyone, be it the players, coaches, referees or fans/parents

**How much do the barriers cost? Do clubs have to use them?**

- The FA has arranged a preferential rate for leagues operating within the Respect programme (£65 per kit)

- They are not obligatory. Clubs can use alternatives if they wish, but the barriers have had a marked effect when employed.

**Have you obtained a grant from the Football Foundation?**

- The Foundation have committed £1m towards funding the touchline barriers for participating leagues.

**What is the role of the Welfare Officer in Respect?**

- All Welfare Officers will promote the Respect programme as part of the measures to create positive football experiences.

- County FA Welfare Officers will provide support and guidance to league and club welfare officers, and assist in dealing with incidents of poor behaviour.

- Youth League Welfare Officers are asked to promote the Respect education programme and assist County Welfare Officers with monitoring and dealing with poor behaviour.

- Club Welfare Officers will help coaches, players and parents understand the Respect measures, ensure that codes are distributed and signed up to, provide guidance on action of the codes are broken, and report any concerns about the welfare of children.

**So overall, how much is really changing?**

- This is a long-term commitment to change a culture within football at all levels. It was important to find consensus across the game on the measures to be adopted.

- We have made meaningful changes which we are confident will have a tangible impact. We won't allow isolated incidents to blow this off-track.

In Section 4 there is a copy of an example of a code of conduct that is used by many clubs. This is the one our club have used for season 2010-2011. Also in Section 4 there is the Zero Tolerance flyer used by Sale United and incorporated by Total Youth Soccer and hopefully many clubs.

The year after the campaign was launched the FA Respect Programme showed it was making great progress (information from FA website):

There has been a 9% increase in the number of qualified referees this season and there are 5,197 trainee referees at Level Nine - I a 45% increase on 2008/09

Dissent cautions are down in 12 out of 16 of the senior professional leagues and divisions. In the Premier League alone dissent cautions are down by 37% whilst in the Championship the numbers are down by 53%, with League One showing an 8% decrease and League Two dropping by 10%

Respect has become a compulsory module in The FA's training courses for all new referees and coaches (over 25,000) coming into the game each season

Referee assaults down 25% on previous season

But there was still work to be done:

800 grassroots games abandoned in 2008/09 season due to player or spectator misconduct

I in 4 parents would not consider confronting an offensive spectator for fear of physical retaliation

The FA's 'Get Into Refereeing' campaign, in association with Carlsberg, aims to recruit a base of over 31,000 registered referees in England by 2012.

*Statistics above from:*

*FA data: Games abandoned due to player or spectator misconduct during 2008/9 season across grassroots football in England.*

*One Poll survey of 2,000 football players and fans (aged 18-45) conducted on 5-7 February 2010.*

The FA's Respect films, entitled 'Are you Losing it?' feature the narratives of an offending player and parent to demonstrate exactly what team mates think about their abusive behaviour. The first film, aimed at adult players, depicts an aggressive 'win at all costs' player and his abusive comments, which are overlaid with the voices of his teammates and their chorus of annoyance and disapproval at his actions. The second film, targeting parents and adult supporters, puts the spotlight on a fresh faced junior player who starts the game with youthful enthusiasm but quickly shrinks in confidence thanks to the overzealous 'support' of their parent.

The FA's approach to the films has been prompted by an ongoing sense of frustration within the grassroots game at the issue of abusive players ruining the game for everyone else.

Taking the Respect message directly to football fans and players, the new films were received at Wembley during the England v Egypt game on 3rd March 2010. The launch of the 'Are you Losing it?' campaign is supported by research findings which suggest that 58% of grassroots players are prepared to call the verbal shots by telling a team mate to calm down if they display offensive behaviour towards an opposing player.

Right at the top of the game in the Premier League, only 3 months after the launch of the campaign, all was not well and Paul Ince, then Blackburn manager, vented his anger:

"There's so much inconsistency, and you wonder why managers get irate. Our jobs are on the line. If they [referees] make a decision that changes the game, then they have got to look at themselves. Talk about the Respect campaign. We're trying to respect them but they've got to start respecting us. It works both ways."

The FA also faced a potential boycott of the Respect campaign in its early days, with at least two Premier League managers reportedly threatening to walk away from the campaign over complaints that disciplinary hearings that season have been a "one-way street".

The campaign had only just begun and was already receiving critics and complaints. If junior coaches were reading this in the nationals in their tea break, then how on earth could the campaign ever filter down to the grassroots football?

# PART ONE

"A Little Respect"
Erasure 1988

## My Story
## Through My Own Eyes and Ears

When I began writing my story, an incident hit the news networks regarding a mass brawl at a pleasant sunny Sunday morning fixture. The referee was assaulted and arrests were made. However, this was not the usual story of half-drunk pub players; amazingly the protagonists were all parents watching a junior fixture! Despite all the good work that is done behind closed doors, or like me, in my own time trying to research and feed the information to the punters who watch the game; it only takes one incident like this to change the public's perception. The good work achieved by the County FA's, Clubs, Officials and schools across the country can feel like it has gone to waste. Incidents like this one can be reported in many national newspapers, reported on TV and plastered all over the internet. The stories may even be read or heard by non-football fans who would be some what disturbed that this 'disease' actually exists in our game in this country.

The story shows how bad it can be, to the point of being humorous. The reality is that such stories will only put off other parents bringing their child to football matches, games and training. And to put off youngsters coming into the game, to officiate, play, coach or help organise.

## Win at all costs...

My coaching career began properly in the summer of 1997, after the pre World Cup tournament in France called 'La Tournoui'. A tournament that seemed meaningless at the time though involved the top four teams in the world, playing an exhibition tournament that was well presented and well organised. You will probably remember this tournament because of the goal that Roberto Carlos struck that immediately entered footballing folklore history – a swerving outside-of-the-foot free-kick.

I set sail to the USA, quite simply, a nervous wreck having had limited experiences of being abroad, never mind living and working there. I'd be okay, I thought on the flight, I've coached my mates (some with big ego's) at 11 a-side and 5 a-side to legend status. I had coached at local clubs and soccer schools and undertaken an old FA preliminary coaching course and had now been recruited by one of the biggest soccer camp companies in the USA. I spent the summer travelling and visiting many states, meeting new people and coaching many children in the United States. The soccer camps are relaxed places, where a parent is merely a taxi driver as they drop off and pick up their child, not observing any of the day other than the presentation on the final day, where Britney or Elvis collect their medal and certificate along with a photo with the coach for the family album.

The Fall came, Autumn in our words, and the start of the real football/soccer season began. My 1st assignment was an Under 11 soccer team in Garden City, Detroit. The experience was one that I was to never forget, and helps me in every day life to achieve, believe and give myself hope.

The team I took on were the typical "Mighty Ducks" team or that of a recent film I would encourage you to watch called Kicking and Screaming where Will Ferris is a busy parent who takes over a team and well, I will let you watch it. By now you get the drift, no hopers to world beaters is cinematic, almost fantasy, though not impossible so it would seem.

This team had never won a game! That's never! They had leaked more goals than a San Marino back line, some weeks into double figures and the twenties. A goal scored was something more rare than my eldest step daughter cleaning her room without being asked. Yes that's rare! Led by a "Soccer Mom"* who coached the team, though needed help and hired the services of a Britannia Soccer coach, my good self.

(*A term commonly used in the US, defined on-line as "a middle-class, suburban woman who spends a significant amount of her time transporting her school-age children to their sporting events or other activities".)

The team was captained by her son who played in goal when the score got out of control (he was also the main striker, midfield general and defender).

The task I was given was pretty simple. The club had hired a coach from the company to get better and maybe win the odd game whilst developing the players.

I looked at the past results to give me an insight, then following a few training sessions I was confident I could put some structure into the team and improve on past performances. My first game saw the team lose 6-1, an improved performance I was told having lost to the Tycoons ten- zip, as they say, last season. This continued; A past 16-4 became 8-3, then a 10-3 became 5-2 and 9-2 became an incredible 1-0 defeat. Though still without a win, the team had organisation, belief and played with improvement and a smile (which to me is the most valuable thing. Former pro, now goalkeeping coach, Gavin Kelly once told me: "as long as they leave with a smile on their face, that is the most important thing.") In the penultimate game of the season, a game previously lost 6-2, the Garden City

Under 11s rose above anything known to them to draw 5-5. A triumph in many ways, with relief that I had helped the team and players improve and develop. The last game was drawn 1-1 and despite the change in fortunes, the news I received was not good.

The Soccer Mom, who had been replaced by myself, was obviously upset and called the company (who were based a million miles away in Washington DC, while I'm in Detroit) to say I was a disaster and the team never wins and all the parents were unhappy.

**"KIRKHAM OUT" she cried, like a lower division season ticket holder.**

The contract with the team was not renewed and a feeling of sadness emerged, but with it came relief, similar to the relief I had felt when drawing 5-5, although that seemed a distant memory. It was over!

I had not succeeded. Personally I don't think Sir Alex, the Special One or the late Sir Bobby Robson would have succeeded, other than to install the same beliefs to the kids I had done.

I had been undermined by a Soccer Mom only wanting to WIN, for her and the parent's pleasure. To WIN to get points, To WIN to rub it in other peoples faces. All the wrong reasons and the American philosophy! Second is for losers and they only breed winners!

The parents were positive throughout during my tenure and most sent messages of support after I moved on, thanking me for the help I had given their children.

The Soccer Mom had missed the real improvement in her team by failing to look beyond the results. The boys now understood positional play. They knew how to pass, control, dribble and shoot correctly. Kicking the ball high was the only technique they had been told. They had learnt communication skills, on and off the field.

They learnt to train together and encourage each other. The players knew things had changed and with it came cards and a medal of thanks for my help. The Soccer Mom as ruthless as a football league chairman giving the gaffer the chop!

Her team had developed quickly, though she hadn't seen it as every time the wheel span, the Jackpot win never arrived - she never saw the improvement. It stays with me now every time I coach and the team I am working with concede a goal. I pick them up, put positives into their heads and encourage them to do things differently and make alternative choices and decisions next time. I don't dress them down, like the opposition manager I recently saw on a Sunday, throwing his bottle Arsene Wenger style. It has shown me that winning is not the key and seeing the players improve and being happy is more important. Unfortunately some parents in our modern game, along with the Soccer Mom, want success instantly, with development taking a less glamorous second place.

Surely it must be better to develop today and win later?

The FA RESPECT campaign has helped and can only improve things in this country. I urge you to read on and as you digest the positive and negative stories and comments, think what you will. Whether you laugh, learn or want to ignore this information, think about how you will react next time you see or hear an incident. Whether you manage, play, officiate, coach or simply watch, this book will change the way you do so forever.

I am by no means the perfect coach, and I'm sure like all coaches out there, I will have my critics. The research into this book has helped me breathe new life into my coaching and changed the way I will operate in the future.

My American dream was shattered though, through my own belief, I would come back to succeed and my stories will unfold as we go on. My eyes have seen too many bad things. My ears heard too many bad stories.

# The Statistics and Dermot Collins

FA figures reported by BBC Radio 5 Live revealed that there have been 330 assaults on referees by amateur footballers in England in 2010, an increase of 27% on the previous year's statistics.

The figures, taken at the end of February, showed that the most serious assaults were down from 8 last year to 3 in that season, but incidents of causing or attempting to cause bodily harm were up from 47 to 53 over the same period.

Most frequent were common assaults, which went up from 205 incidents to 276 in a year. Common assault includes barging and pushing – the sort of behaviour that is often seen on an adult football pitch, but not usually towards referees in junior games.

Whilst the FA were "concerned" at the figures, they have been keen to point out that, with 35,000 matches happening in England every weekend, assaults of this nature are still extremely rare.

I spent an afternoon contacting every FA County in England asking them 4 direct questions about the Respect campaign. Peter Ducksbury from the FA's Respect campaign responded to me to explain that my e-mail had been forwarded to Dermot Collins from the FA and he would reply with answers. Dermot did so and sent me details of the work done with the Respect campaign. I thank him for his contribution. If you google him, you will find many interviews with Collins and his work is going well.

"I deplore any assault on a referee, but we've got to say that this isn't the experience of most referees in this country," said Dermot Collins, the FA's Respect Manager.

"We surveyed 4,000 referees across 15,000 games this season and they mark their experiences as four out of five. Most referees have a great experience of the game."

"When we launched the Respect programme in 2008 we always acknowledged we were up against a pretty significant problem. We were looking to change some pretty well established and engrained poor behaviour and that's what we have been doing".

Indeed, FA statistics published in January 2011 showed a 29% increase in the number of male referees (26,889) and a 31% increase in the number of female referees (853) involved in the national game since the Respect programme was introduced in 2008.

Statistics also show that dissent cautions across the top four divisions of English football we were down by 9% in 2009-10 compared to the season before.

Whether that figure represents a true reduction in dissent or an increased level of tolerance from referees in the professional game is a point of debate.

Indeed, some observers believe that poor behaviour in the grassroots game will not be fully addressed while professional players and managers continue to set a bad example.

**"I recognise that," said Collins, "but we don't see referees being chased around the car park at The Emirates or Old Trafford."**

"The power of example in the professional game is very, very powerful, but when we talk about assaults on referees, that is not happening in the professional game. I think it's one of those issues that grassroots football has got to look at."

Premier League players shouting at referees may foster a culture of disrespect throughout football – while media hype and analysis around refereeing mistakes does little to help – but do those of us involved at the grassroots have a right to moan about the professional game unless we also do our part?

This is our game, so shouldn't we all have a responsibility for our own behaviour and that of our team mates? Collins certainly believes so.

He concluded:

"I work for the FA but I'm also a coach, I'm a team captain, I'm a club chairman and, in all of those roles, I've got a chance to influence the way that people behave towards referees. That's really what we have got to do throughout football."

# Why does Junior Football Needs Respect?

The Football Association responded to a plea that ultimately stemmed from the ongoing problems with grassroots football, as they endeavoured to tackle the unacceptable behaviour that was growing on the touchlines and on pitches all over the country. The media were homing in on the troubles and the FA quite simply had to respond.

The drop out of referees, young players, coaches and parent volunteers, was on the increase due to the abuse that was killing our game. The rising levels led to some disturbing statistics which were collated and printed all over the press. The media seemed to enjoy the periling stories that emerged and with it came newspaper articles that shocked the nation.

Respect aimed to bring the fun back for all children playing the game. Rather than allowing parental pressure, often driven by the parents own personal pride and enjoyment, to ruin the fun. The campaign aims to fight this negative impact and reports now being published suggest some positive signs.

The FA has been running its Respect campaign with positive results and current data indicates that progress is being made in local leagues and junior football. Some of this progress has been evidenced by the recently published statistics on the FA's "Are you losing it" website:

"There are about 25,000 affiliated referees in the country and although this is almost at an all-time low, this number has improved since the FA's respect campaign was launched, and in addition the number of referees being newly qualified has also gone up. Despite these promising figures thousands of referees are still quitting football on a regular basis and many children are being lost to football because of pushy and over enthusiastic parents."

The FA's respect campaign targeted pushy parents and this book highlights their bad practice along with the positive ways clubs have responded.

In junior football, parents need to be accountable for their actions on the sidelines. Parents' win at all costs – 'my boy/girl is a star' attitude is strangling the youth game, not only giving it a damaging name among other sports but also discouraging talented children from taking part. The biggest issue is that often the parents do not realise they are the ones doing it.

The problems encountered constantly are parents/coaches pushing their own child too much; instilling a win at all costs attitude; and in doing so showing no respect towards the officials administering the laws of the game. The issues seen too frequently in junior football are twofold: 1) players are often excluded because their skills and talents have not developed sufficiently to be deemed able to make a winning impact on the team 2) parents pushing and expecting too much of their own children.

These problems offer a huge challenge and the FA Respect campaign aims to confront these issues head-on. Many clubs have applied to become FA Charter Standard clubs and in doing so have agreed to abide by a set of codes of conduct, which are targeted towards coaches, parents and the players themselves. The codes of conduct which have already been explained require all involved in football to show respect.

Codes of conduct provide a set of rules for all involved in football to follow, but the question is: Are they being adhered to? Evidence shows us that even when clubs have a signed declaration, which the parent has read and understood, they are often ignoring the guidelines within them.

Below the FA has offered a few suggestions on how to embed the codes of conduct and the message from the Respect campaign into the minds of all involved in football. They suggest these statements below should be repeated before every game:

- Referee is in charge
- Encourage team-mates
- Shout, but don't criticise
- Play fairly
- Enjoy the game
- Captain only speaks to the referee
- Try whatever the score

The junior football coach is the key person and the behaviour of the coach on the sidelines sets the tone for both the players and supporters. They have the ability to ensure, to a certain extent, the attitude of the parents watching. It's obvious that if the coaches are over-enthusiastic and pushy from the sidelines, then the parents watching will consider it the norm and do likewise. If, however, the coach is calm shows an appropriate level of encouragement and doesn't shout excessively, then the parents will follow this example.

Coaches have a duty to ensure that parents understand the boundaries when watching and encouraging their team and that they should abide by the clubs codes of conduct.

Football is a game which is played to win and the satisfaction that winning brings is obvious; though it should not be played to win at all costs, excluding those players who are not deemed skilful enough. The enjoyment of football is not only in the winning but also in the taking part.

The majority of junior football is played without a league appointed referee. This means that most of our games are refereed by a club official or a parent. Quite often the referee will have not attended any formal training, and is giving up his or her time to officiate the match. This puts undue strain on the referee (parent), especially with both sets of supporters expecting the non-appointed official to be as good as a paid professional referee from the Premier League.

Both teams expect a referee to be able to make the correct decision every time, especially when they deem the decision to be in their team's favour, and they are annoyed when a decision is given against their team. Often abuse is directed towards the referee for giving an "incorrect" decision in the eyes of the parent. The coach can in some cases be the first person to aim abuse at the referee with the parents following suit…taking their cue from the coach.

The referee's job is to record the details of the match, apply the laws of the game and keep a close view on the events taking place on the pitch, as well as having an overall awareness of the game itself. Doing this is a skill and is learnt through training and practice.

**To ask a parent to referee any football match and then to expect them to get every decision right every time is lunacy.**

Unfortunately, some parents, who have little understanding of how difficult it is to effectively referee a football match, feel the need to give abuse to both players and referees. Such parents can only be described as ignorant and are an unwelcome part of youth football.

Once again this is where the football coach must lead by taking the attitude that whatever the decision, the referee is an integral part of the game and must be respected. The attitude of the coach will rub off on the parents, leaving the referee some freedom to officiate without fear of making mistakes.

The FA's Respect campaign addresses touchline behaviour, attempting to protect our children from over enthusiastic parents, while allowing our referees to officiate without fear or reprisals.

Visit the FA's Respect website for more information. I hope this book helps the FA with its cause and the dream to eradicate this infected generation of problematic spectators.

## Who'd be a Referee?

Poor decisions by Referees give parents the chance to air their views. In fact it's a minefield out there for the refs. Young Referees, of 14 years old perhaps, are berated throughout a torturous hour of football. People will cringe at what goes on. I feel this is something that will only decrease when it is addressed at the top. With major incidents in football being highlighted in the media 24/7, there is plenty of opportunity for debate and to consider the issue of respect towards match officials.

A typical weekend for me would be to coach and watch our local players and teams; then watch the Premier League games in the afternoon.

The Last Word (on Sky Sports) offers a chance to review the big talking points. On the way to work on a Monday morning, again the incidents are highlighted by radio phone-ins and a referee is often interviewed on the weekend topic that has become headline news. The tabloids front and back page highlight a sending off, a bad tackle or reckless lunge. After Rafeal saw red for Manchester United at Spurs on January 17th in a live sky sports game, the front page and back page covered the story, leading with NO RESPECT!

Rafeal lost his cool when referee Mike Dean decided his trip on Benoit Assou-Ekotto was enough for a second booking. The United youngster clearly disagreed and faced a charge of improper conduct. He later apologised.

That Sunday saw a whole host of other games…

What about the cracking game at Anfield? The stale mate itself at White Hart Lane? The Midlands derby? The Tyneside derby? Yeah, they all featured, but the media focused on the red card incident at the lane highlighting further the problems within the game!

The negative sides to the game provide talking points, yes, however the knock-on effect is that parents then look to our grassroots Sunday football for more talking points.

**"Should he have been sent off?" "Why did that parent run on and push the keeper?" "The coach is rubbish and needs the boot!" (though gives up his time voluntary as no one else will do it!)**

It pours onto our pitches. It happens in the Premier League so why not at Grassroots!

Mums, Dads and Grandparents shout and march up and down touchlines as though their life depends on it, berating the official *"the referee's s\*\*t"* all inspired by reports of so-called bad refereeing in the media.

The Dads marching up and down the line waving imaginary flags every time it may be offside or out of play. Does this remind you of anyone you that know?

One story on a forum from the BBC told of a dad who once held a pair of scissors to a boy's throat as his team led 5-0 informing him, that any more goals and he would get it!

## Mini Soccer, the way forward?

At Mini Soccer, a game played without the competitive element of scores and league tables, the referee is meant to be invisible. "Not even there" they say "just get on with the flow of play". With league titles, relegation, promotion and Cups at stake, referees become visible and everyone wants to be heard.

New directives that are being engineered aim to eradicate much of negative side of junior football and produce a whole new breed of players and parents (we live in hope!).

Visiting a tournament for Under 7s in 2010, at Hull City, all parents and players were shown a video about Respect and the Respect PowerPoint presentation was shown before the players went out to play.

All games played were mini games with no scores kept and no referees as the coaches made all of the calls. Of course, with many Premier League officials floating about, this was done in a respectable manner (the teams were also hand picked and invite only). The question is:

Would this work on a bigger stage, on parks and pitches across the country?

It should and at times it should be tried, applied and worked on.

Up to any age, with no league tables kept but merely fixtures, as is demonstrated at School of Excellence level. It may be here quicker than we know it with the FA's new Future Game programme.

The kids will learn to play and express themselves in the correct manner and not have to listen to parents screaming, shouting and disrupting the play.

Some leagues have already taken this approach. The FA are to introduce new and exciting directives, which have been designed to develop formats of football that will allow players the chance to play in a structure that will give them the best opportunity to reach their potential and stay within the game.

Under 7s and 8s already do not play in leagues due to the FA rules and this has had its critics. Some parents and coaches don't understand why there are no points or tables at this age group and are over heard saying its stupid!

**"What's the point in playing?" you hear.**

The point is simple; by having no points, you have time to nurture the player's development. However, I'm sad to say that in my time I have witnessed plenty of incidents at Under 7s and 8s matches, as some of the parents, new to this side of the game, are already falling into bad habits and want to win too much.

Following a case study it was concluded that:

"Young people were not interested in over–zealous competition and placed the emphasis on participation. Young people are not satisfied with what they see as inappropriate adult concern for results and performance"
(MacPhail et al. 2003)

So if a 14-18 year old is 'not bothered' why on earth will a 7 year old be?

The FA's directives are a step in the right direction and after the fall out of the World Cup in South Africa 2010, the English game is again under review (and scrutiny from the media!).

Why do we have competitive leagues, play 11 a-side at Under 11 on massive pitches, when a boy or girl of 11 can't even reach the crossbar? The Spanish and other European top dogs do things different and play smaller side games and I think the change to 9 versus 9 will create a better environment all round.

Will people be up for the change? Will you be up for the change if or when it happens? How will you react and will it change your views? Do you believe in getting the best out of the young players we train, coach and watch?

Football, as we know it, needs to change the picture and give a better impression to the outside world.

## Ashley Cole and Little Johnny...

Months before the Respect campaigns official launch, Ashley Cole, a top England defender from Chelsea, had made a mockery of respect when he faced up to referee Mike Riley in March 2008.

Cole turned his back on Riley, which was deemed a clear act of public dissent and belittling a referee. The player, already on a caution, made a horror tackle on Spurs defender Alan Hutton. An outcry of support came for Riley from his peers as Keith Hackett backed by others hit back at Cole. Hackett's concerns were that children copy their heroes and he felt really strongly about this case and explained that respect needs to start at the top. A massive global audience had gathered to watch this game as Chelsea and Tottenham played out a highly entertaining (though fiery at times) 4-4 draw. Though, it was to be Riley who paid for his apparent lack of control and was demoted by the Premier League.

If Cole is doing this, then why shouldn't Little Johnny from our local junior club do it? Imagine - the junior football club's coach came out in the local press and defended Little Johnny just as the Chelsea gaffer did at the time. The junior coach wrote in his report that he submits to the local paper about the decision. The paper writes it and then who looks the mug? The ref who has been insulted!

The fans read it and say "Yeah, Riley was wrong" likewise the followers of the junior football club read in the local paper that the young 14 year old referee was wrong, he must be as it says so in black and white.

Cole and Little Johnny are now the victims and become heroes to their following and life goes on, with another incident waiting to happen. Cole is not alone in this, and if he ever reads this then I apologise to him, though he must be a daft lad for allegedly cheating on Mrs Cole!

Little Johnny will never read it as he is purely fictional, even though he is often referred to in football dialogue. Poor Little Johnny!

The Respect campaign is being pioneered in the Premier League. It has to work, and does to a degree.

The Rafeal incident was compared with that of Cole's (sorry Ashley again!) and Alex Ferguson, his manager and master of the media, said:

"I don't need to discuss the sending off. I don't need to speak about referees, it's out of bounds now Thank God! "

Fergie had, had previous against Mike Dean (the referee that day) which landed him a £10,000 fine and two match touch line ban for improper conduct. Steven Howard wrote in The Sun the day after that "Fergie would have gone through the roof in the old days."

Months later, in March 2011, the most successful manager ever in the Premier League was banned for 5 games for showing no respect to a referee – so maybe Fergie isn't yet completely reformed!

Unfortunately, the old days that Steven Howard wrote about are those that some parents still bring to touchlines. The *"you won't change me"* attitude. *"I know how to watch football, and I will stand were the F\*\*K I like"* (as I was told by a visiting parent one season, busy coaching his boy in goal - well actually berating his son's "SHAMBOLIC" performance (to quote the Dad), to the point where the lad cried and had to be replaced, though it didn't stop there as his dad dragged him into the car park for what looked like an early night. The boy in question was only seven years old. Not old enough to have any experience at all, though he was expected to pull off saves like Ben Foster or Joe Hart).

# Setting an example...

Football is so available to people these days with 24-hour sports news channels, with fine websites and matches from all around the world being shown almost every day. With more football discussion shows than ever before, there has become a faux intellectualism about football tactics because people need more to talk about.

At the time of compiling the information for this book, Manchester United (the team I support) were in the news again as Wayne Rooney hit the headlines in a 2-4 victory against West Ham. However, not for scoring a hat trick that dragged his team from 2-0 down to 4-2 up at Upton Park.

In the previous week, Respect had been on everyone's lips as the Premier League chief executive Richard Scudamore announced a crackdown on the "unacceptable" behaviour by players and managers. Only days later Rooney ran to a live Sky Sports camera to swear to the nation, children and parents alike. This was predictably met with headlines the following day that must have made those involved in the Respect campaign simply cringe.

It was not the first time Rooney had shown disrespect in this way after shouting into cameras and slating the England crowd in the World Cup following a drab 0-0 draw with Algeria.

Following the incident at Upton Park, Wayne apologised blaming the high intensity of the game and insisted it wasn't meant to upset anyone, in particular parents and children.

Rooney's name appears on the back of many child's shirts whether England or Manchester United, he has a duty to be a role model. He along with others let themselves down in the face of adversity.

Wayne continued to remark that he had been the first player to be banned for swearing and won't be the last to make such an outburst. Swearing is a culture that is part of our game. Ryan Giggs, a United legend, commented on Football 365 the next day that he was simply "bamboozled" by the ban and the club also issued statement expressing their dismay.

The FA were forced into thinking of some form of punishment, a task they did not welcome but one which occupied them for over a week. There was all manner of fuss. He was banned for two games including an FA Cup semi final they subsequently lost against arch rival Manchester City.

Who is to blame? Make your own mind up....

# The Soccer Parent

They want their child to be the next Jack Wilshire, Gareth Bale or Wayne Rooney...
They are willing to fight for it.
In December 2007, ahead of the Respect campaign, David Harrison from the Daily Telegraph reported on the parents who are turning the beautiful game ugly.

Harrison reported on a match in Surrey involving two teams of nine-year-old boys. The game was evenly poised at 1-1 and less than 10 minutes remained. Around 20 parents had gathered on the touchlines to cheer on their offspring. Harrison describes the action as it unfolds...

"A fair-haired youngster in a red strip dribbles the ball down the right wing and heads towards the goal. But his charge for glory is halted abruptly when a burly opponent in royal blue rushes over and sends him crashing to the ground with a heavy tackle.
The referee signals a foul. An argument breaks out and, less than a minute later, the playing field echoes to the sickening sound of human head on human nose."

However, Harrison points out that neither the aggressor nor the victim was wearing a football strip. The father of the "burly opponent" had taken offence when the fouled player's dad had objected to the tackle. The attacker, a burly man in his thirties, had to be restrained then dragged away by other parents, whilst still shouting abuse.

With the victim left cleaning his bloodied nose, the referee decided to abandon the match, leaving the children bemused and disappointed. Their fun well and truly over.

Harrison reported that this was not an isolated incident but part of an alarming trend up and down the country. Assaults in junior football are not only becoming more frequent but also more violent, with spectators, often parents, the main offenders. One quoted source said:

"It's madness out there. We have parents fighting with each other and punching referees and linesmen. Coaches get involved, too. Sometimes it's the mothers who start the fights - and they can be worse than the men. It's ruining the game and it's terrible that this is happening in front of the children."

The Surrey FA had even written to all clubs following a record number of abandoned matches. One disillusioned coach summed it up:

**"The game kicks off and then the parents kick off."**

Harrison highlighted others incidents across the country which included not only the shockingly violent but also some bizarre and childish examples.

"In Huddersfield, a linesman at an under-13s game was beaten unconscious by a 40-year-old woman and a 16-year-old youth...In rural Somerset, fights have broken out after opposition parents have tripped up seven-year-old players as they ran down the wing...In sleepy Wiltshire, a father, opting for a crude but non-violent protest, drove a 4x4 vehicle onto the pitch and refused to move until the referee changed a decision."

You would have thought that matches involving younger children were less likely to attract problems. However, the opposite is often true. Parents are more likely to bring their children to the match and will inevitably stay and watch. However, the competitive instinct soon kicks-in. A child welfare officer in the West Midlands was quoted as saying:

"They are living their dreams through their children, they think their kid could be the next superstar. They want little Johnny to win at all costs. It means they are totally wound up during the games and they can just lose it when they get frustrated if Johnny makes a mistake, someone kicks him, or the ref gives what they consider to be a bad decision."

There he is again, Little Johnny!

A child's confidence can be severely damaged by parental behaviour, not only on the pitch but also socially in the wider world. It is difficult to develop skills in a pressure cooker atmosphere, when it is easier to punt the ball forward than try a new skill or trick. Experts have said that it is no co-incidence that good home-grown English players are an exception and the national side consistently underperforms. As Kelly Simmons, the FA's head of football development says "[the parents] don't seem to realise how much damage they are doing to their children."

Inevitably, finding people to officiate in this atmosphere is becoming increasingly difficult. In the year before Harrison wrote his article, the FA reported that 7,000 referee's quit. John Tuppin, of the Durham County FA was quoted as saying:

"Quite apart from the threat of physical violence, they have to put up with shocking language and abuse, I've seen a lot of young refs walk off the pitch in tears. Finding young referees and training them is not a problem; keeping them is. They think that refereeing games of seven- to 10-year-olds will be a fun thing to do on a Sunday morning. And it should be. But then they find themselves being screamed at by some loudmouthed parent on the touchline. It's no wonder they ask themselves, 'Is it worth the hassle?'?"

Referee's assistants are also targets and their proximity to the crowd makes them even more vulnerable. One parent reported giving up after being punched, whilst in a similar incident at an under 15s match, a parent was fined a total of £1,450 following an assault.

In response to some of these incidents, some leagues introduced precursors to what would become the Respect Barriers mentioned at the beginning of the book. One of the early adopters was the Wigan Youth League where the number of abandoned matches fell from 15 to just one after the introduction of barriers.

The FA took note of what was happening, leading to the launch of the Respect campaign. The thinking behind the Respect campaign was summed up perfectly by Paul Cooper, a football coach and the founder of Give Us Back Our Game.

"We have to end the adult-driven 'win at all costs' philosophy. Children just want to play, and they can organise themselves and enjoy themselves. We need a change of culture. Adults have taken over the children's game and use it for their own purposes. We have to give it back to the children."

## My Story (Reprise I)

My American dream did become more enterprising and with it came a wealth of experience which led to employment within the football industry in the United Kingdom, through professional clubs, junior clubs and schools.

Whilst in Michigan I succeeded enough to be promoted to an area director for the summer camps (soccer schools in the UK) and developed into a stronger coach and more assertive leader. I achieved so much in the years I spent over the water and although winning is not the key to development, the differences in American culture (coupled with my experiences) taught me how to blend a winning mentality with developmental coaching.

LA Forza soccer club will always be close to my heart, along with the people, friends and coaches I met. Coaching a successful girls team to a Michigan title and watching them progress further to Olympic development teams was a real joy. I worked with a fantastic Under 17 High School girl's team, who responded to everything I coached them. The two boy's teams I worked with at Under 10 and 12 were a pleasure to watch and became better players over my tenure.

The parents understanding of the game of football at the time in the late 90s was not as clear as a parent here in the UK. The American game is baseball or American football, though it is changing since the arrival of Mr Beckham on their shores and the Major Soccer League has been given more attention.

A long clearance was met with a round of applause and a short pass that began an attacking move saw them less animated. I spent a day at another club helping develop their coaching curriculum and coaching ethos, sessions and planning.

The evaluation saw questions from the coaches and I was met with "Coach Chris, what exactly is a corner kick, we have no idea?"

That shows the difference. The parents here in the UK know the corner kick inside out, and query why Under 8s don't practice set pieces, demonstrating a different knowledge and understanding.

I don't have many recollections of major parental sideline incidents, though I do remember a dad remonstrating with me when I gave so-called weaker boys starts in the team. On one occasion a parent called me on my mobile whilst I was coaching to inform me: *"if Jack didn't go on and that load of s\*\*t didn't come off"*, then he would be leaving with Jack and finding another team. At the time I didn't bow down to his demands and didn't replace the players in question, as they needed the playing time to develop. Jack's dad just wanted to win, no matter how. We did however win the game two-zip, and everyone in the 16 player squad played the same allotted playing time. All went home happy, except Jack's dad who was frothing at the mouth! Jack was embarrassed and apologised to me at training while his father decided to send me to Coventry (or the US equivalent of the industrial midlands city!).

The boys developed all season and hand in hand became a stronger team. To just rely on Jack, and give no others a chance is unfair and wrong, though I fear it still happens all over the place as we speak.

The Americans did not tolerate bad behaviour at any of their tournaments, though I have had read some horror stories from the States since returning home. A parent, so dejected that his boy wasn't in the team, decided one day that he would spike the drinks of the best players so his son would get more playing time. Unfortunately for him, all the boys including his own drank the mixture and were all violently sick on the pitch, so badly that the game had to be called to an abrupt end. The dad was later jailed for his antics.

The Yanks have many interesting ideas of fair play and I saw several examples of this at the large competitions. Sin bins were in operation, like in ice hockey, for any perpetrators of foul play. I took a Child Protection certificate over there and the training group was shown clips of a tournament in California which looked wonderful, with great goals, passes, delightful touchlines (we thought!) and all played in a respectful manner. Over 156 teams from all over the States attended at different ages, as did 58 recognised and registered paedophiles from the state! So in saying that, you never know who is on your touchline and it emphasised the importance of safeguarding in youth football. Despite media suggestions that checking can be heavy-handed and unnecessary, the dangers are very real.

Parent issues were helped in the operation by each team at La Forza having a parent manager who dealt with all the issues, admin stuff and the like. The coach was then left to concentrate on what they do best, and not be sidelined by the issues surrounding the team. This certainly helped and gave us a platform to succeed.

The summer camps gave us joy, the seasons a lot of satisfaction, I longed for a similar position in the UK and in 2001 came home to England to begin looking for coaching positions.

I was to be astonished with what I witnessed and had to tolerate on my return.

# Part Two

**Why does it always rain on me? – Travis 1999**

## The Media

The media can attract unfortunate press to any situation; none more so than a parent ruining a junior football match. The adverse publicity that crops up from these stories gives the reporters another chance to take a swipe at football.

> **"In six years coaching my son's football team I have come to the following conclusion: short of excess intake of alcohol, there is nothing that alters the behaviour of adults for the worse as much as youth football."**

That is the amazing judgement reached by Jim White. White writes humorous and insightful sports analysis in the Daily Telegraph. He is also a prolific author, broadcaster and journalist who has written a bestseller on youth football – "You can't win anything with kids". His book is a great read and I would strongly recommend it to any parent coach coming into the game.

White became disillusioned after spending umpteen weekends witnessing grown men and women shouting at children, screaming at officials and generally showing less maturity than the eight year olds on the pitch. The coaches, usually a player's dad in White's experience, were identified as the main culprits, with White calling the result "little short of child abuse".

We have seen several examples of appalling behaviour already in this book but White adds to the hall of shame with a tale of a young

seven year old opponent publicly humiliated after conceding a penalty for a clumsy handball. The coach screamed abuse at the player, calling him amongst other things "fat, useless and stupid" until the young boy fled from the pitch in tears, finding a safe haven on the branch of a tree where he remained for the rest of the match. Did the coach calm down and apologise? No, "Good riddance," he shouted "We're better off without you, you useless tosser."
White concluded:

**"For too many small boys their experience of the beautiful game will be limited to red-faced coaches and snarling parents. No wonder once they reach adulthood, they are giving up football in droves. Our generation should be ashamed"**

In April 2008, Sky Sports News focused on the troubles with a Special Report on the "State of the Game" with an investigation which looked at dilapidated grassroots facilities across the country. They also focused on the problems caused by bad behaviour on the touchlines.

More youngsters give up playing football in England than any other country in Europe and one of the major causes for this high drop-out rate is down to pressure and abuse from the touchlines.

Sports Minister Gerry Sutcliffe at the time expressed his concerns stating that more must be done to ensure parents understand not to put too much pressure on their kids. He said: "Parents have got to understand that at a very young age - and I go to watch my grandson play who's eight - that they shouldn't be subjected to the sort of pressure that they are. Again, we've got to try and work with the FA and the leagues to make sure they understand that."

The Sky report highlighted the games being abandoned due to touchline trouble. That season in 2008, 38 youth clubs in Birmingham had been reported for touchline disturbances; 14 games had been abandoned in Lancashire and 14 in Manchester, yet the season had still not finished.

Referees became victims of over-zealous and aggressive supporters and many have been forced to give up the game in fear.

I watched the report at the time and watched again before putting this book together.

## Junior football in the Midlands…

In March 2008 local journalist Warren Manger wrote about the state of junior football in the Midlands. He had found parents in Coventry and Warwickshire were bringing disgrace to local children's football games and the touchline behaviour was so bad that six matches in the Coventry Minor League had to be abandoned. Games involving children as young as eight were being disrupted by parents shouting and screaming at referees and opposition players.

In my own experience the most problems that have occurred are at the youngest of age groups. In 2007 the FA made a decision that no child under 8 would play for points or play in a league (as previously mentioned). This was met with, a huge public outcry of "Why can our kids not compete for medals and trophies like the older kids "

The simple fact of the matter was that the medals and trophies caused the problems. The desire at 6 years old, spurred on by a parent living their child's dreams. At this age, children are just into infant school and busy learning how to count, spell and do things for themselves. However, they also expected to play football: score; tackle; defend leads; and ultimately put trophies on the mantelpiece.

**At an under seven game I witnessed in 2010, the coach was approached several times and "offered" into the car park by parents.**

The parents were ruthless and accused the referee of cheating to win 3 points. Three points that in fact were not on offer during this arranged fixture which is now classed as a friendly!

The aggression also caused the youngsters to become more violent. Their tackles changed and the whole situation was embarrassing for the players involved and led to complaints from the home club, who quite rightly sent a report to league officials. The club concerned contacted the offending club to see if anything had been done but they only received confirmation of the complaints and they said they didn't expect an outcome when I followed up the lead.

They did comment after this incident that if they were asked to play the same opposition again, they would refuse. That's where it's at, and we are talking about 6 year olds!

I ran a World Cup tournament in 2006, to coincide with the real deal. Over 60 participants took part, which gave us 10 teams of six-a-side and a brilliant month of tournaments played in a great sporting manner. Players and parents enjoyed alike, though the one thing I remember were the tears in the eyes of the losing competitors owing to the degree of eagerness to win a medal. On reflection, in 2010 we ran a similar competition and all children received the same reward, no scores were kept, no winners, no losers, just awards for fair play and improving performances.

Going back into the Midlands, a teenage player was reported to have assaulted a referee. The Coventry area at the time had been branded as the worst in the whole West Midlands which shocked local officials. Derrick May, secretary of Coventry Minor League, said: "Our record this season is a disgrace. The sport I love is being ruined. People have simply got to show more respect to the referees."

Since reading this, I researched Derrick Mays comments further; he was clearly upset and rightly so. I felt it was positive that he had come out and given everyone involved a public dressing down. Some leagues hide behind it, or brush it under the carpet. They issue a monthly newsletter which highlights the incidents, though it never reaches the real eyes and ears it should do. May was dismayed that the parents were killing the game he loved.

Aggressive and foul-mouthed parents in Coventry and Warwickshire were forcing referees to abandon children's football matches and six matches in the Coventry Minor Football League have been stopped already that season because of abuse and threats aimed at officials. A 15-year-old player was eventually charged with assault on a referee following a fateful Sunday morning youth match. The shocking problem also extends into adult football where five referees were allegedly been attacked by angry players and spectators at matches in Coventry, Nuneaton and Stratford.

Derrick May issued a statement "We have had more games abandoned than any other youth league in the region." He continued "It appears to me that some parents think they can store up all the frustration from their jobs and homes during the week and take it out on the referee at the weekend. I was watching a game in the park the other week and the man next to me told me he had taken his son out of the local football team and started him playing rugby instead because they teach more discipline and respect towards referees."

John Morris, recruiting officer for the Coventry Referees' Association, said: "The referee often gets lambasted because they are an easy target. But not all the shouting is directed at the referee. There is also a lot of built-in aggression in the way parents shout at the children too, like frustrated former footballers who can't play the game anymore."

Mr May said physical threats to referees at youth matches had decreased but general hostility towards referees continued and included basic courtesy.

"Very few teams welcome referees when they arrive - they are just left waiting on their own until the match starts, we are trying to encourage teams in our league to welcome the referee and not to leave them hanging around waiting to be paid afterwards because that is when any aggrieved parents are likely to come and have a go at them."

The media were in a frenzy with it all and even top flight managers were having their say. QPR manager Neil Warnock writes a weekly column for the Independent in which he told us of his son William playing at under-nine level, which is eight-a-side, for Crystal Palace at Arsenal's home venue.

It may not be the Premier League but people take these matches very seriously. The U11s and U13s also played: the U11s lost but the U13s, having been losing, scored two late goals to win. Neil looked across and all he could see were parents running down the touchline like aircraft with their arms out wide.

**"It was one of the funniest things I've ever seen" remarked Warnock.**

Kenny Dalglish came back into the game to save Liverpool's 2011 season. Soon into the job he was interviewed by the Sunday Mirror, and said "It's about time, some people began to respect the Respect campaign." He was keen that his club, Liverpool, adhered to the campaign and respected officials. He said "We will try our best to retain our dignity and show respect to referees, but we would also like to think they give us the respect we deserve by at least trying to go along with the guidelines of the campaign"

# THE DISRESPECT TIMES

## Touchline aggression is all too common, say parents.

One local press office was driven to canvass opinion amongst spectators, such was the local focus on the issue, with many admitting that adult violence at children's matches was common. Here is what some of them thought:

"It was parents against parents."

"There are occasions when the parents get frustrated and have a go at the ref - it's a free country - but it should be stopped."

On the suggestion of what would become the Respect Barriers, parents said:

"I think a safe zone would be sad - that we have to segregate people because of possible violence that might occur to the referee".

Another parent was in favour, adding: "Quite often the linesmen have to fight against the crowd. It would keep people that can be a little bit loud a metre away from the lads that are on the pitch."

Another suggestion was: "A rule should be brought in to say only positive things should be shouted to the players on the pitch from the side line."

Already set up in neighbouring Birmingham in 2008, another Respect campaign was being hailed as a success. Local FA statistics showed that 12 fewer matches had been abandoned and assaults on referees were down.

Mike Fellows, discipline secretary at Birmingham FA, said: "Four years ago we had a lot of referees being abused, especially young referees but things have got a lot better since we launched our big Respect the Referee campaign."

Birmingham's Respect the Referee initiative introduced a zero-tolerance approach to players and spectators who abuse referees.
This included naming and shaming abusive footballers on the Birmingham County FA's website and in local newspapers.
Other measures have included:

- Making abusive players responsible for their fines instead of the clubs.
- Forcing fans of both teams to stand on the same touchline to stop them arguing across the pitch.
- Roping off pitches to keep parents and spectators away from the touchlines and stop them encroaching on the pitch.

Mr Fellows said that when the Central Warwickshire Youth League considered roping off pitches the local council workers had raised safety concerns that other park users could trip over the plastic stakes and injure themselves! Unbelievable.

Birmingham County FA's "Respect the Ref" Campaign aimed to address the drop-out rate of Match Officials by encouraging everyone to play their part in ensuring Referees are able to do their job without fear of intimidation and the Birmingham Evening Mail was a major supporter of the campaign.

# THE DISREPECT TIMES

## Junior tournament erupts into violence

A JUNIOR football tournament in was marred by violence one Saturday, after a fight broke out between opposing sets of supporters.

The manager of an under 12s junior team was taken to hospital with severe cuts and bruises to his head following the brawl.

The violence caused the match to be abandoned and both teams were subsequently kicked out of the tournament - which was being hosted by a Junior Football Club.

The club chairman said: 'In all my years of junior football, I have never seen anything like that. We have been running this tournament for five years and we have never had a problem like this.'

'The tournament is organised for the children, for their enjoyment. And I asked all the parents at the start to remember that and to respect the refereeing decisions. For this to then happen is disgraceful.'

A lot of coordinating goes into these supposedly fun days.

One idiot can ruin everything for everybody!

cont...

The football tournament attracted 120 teams that weekend and involved over 1,000 children between the ages of 8 and 14 years-of-age.

It is unclear why the fighting broke out but following the violence the organisers were adamant both teams had to go.

The club said: "I decided the best thing was for them to leave and all the other clubs agreed with me. It had been a brilliant day before that. We had even had comments from Everton scouts that it was the best organised tournament they had ever been to. But for that to happen was a disgrace."

*Excerpts of the report above taken from the Stockport Express.*

Another coach reported, after he had won a local tournament at Under 8 level by beating the hosts in the final, that he was surprised by the actions of the opposition. Winning is something that needs to be honoured by both coaches and this then can rub off on the kids. Instead the parent coach, after losing 5-2, marched his team and refused to shake the reporting coaches hand. He declined to attend the presentation which was held by the local mayor. His runners up medals seemingly to be passed on. His Under 8 team, will have undoubtedly been upset at losing the final, though it was then the coaches role to use his adult common sense. Instead he ran off like a coward, and probably went home to wash over where he went wrong.

His team will know no different and how can they learn to lose properly if this is going on at Under 8 level? All this when Under 8s aren't supposed to be playing competitive football anyway!

**"If you tolerate this then your children will be next!"** –
**Manic Street Preachers, 1998**

## 2. Pushy Parents:
## Are pushy parents spoiling football matches?

In March 2007 BBC's Football Focus and Radio 5 Live along with
606 (the popular weekend phone in) asked for stories of soccer
mums and dads on touchlines on their site as the problems began to
become more apparent with wider use of the internet, forums and
blogs. More people were being made aware of this culture that was
becoming a menace within the game we love. Magazines and
newspapers waded in with their views, and the dreadful stories
began to mount up. Their website actually crashed due to the
volume of interest.

Referees, spectators, parents, and coaches replied in their droves
and although there was little disagreement that passion is important
in any participation sport, many have asked whether that passion
from the sidelines, goes too far and affects the way the players
perform.

Unlike the Premier League, junior football clubs were not trying
to compete in the same way as the global stars. The people involved
needed to realise that the game is primarily a children's activity and a
completely different concept to adult professional football.
Therefore behaviour must be adapted accordingly.

It looked like a documentary was going to be made as the BBC
had also asked for videos and pictures to go with the stories. I have
long thought a documentary would be a great idea and if anyone
from the BBC is looking to make one, then I'm sure it would make
interesting viewing. Much like the dodgy builder, plumber and
mechanic programmes. Perhaps the thought of being chased around

car parks after filming some angry parent doesn't appeal to them, though I'm sure the viewer would be entertained, if not amazed!

I have taken a selection of stories from the BBC forums and Sky Sports blogs which reflected the balance of opinion they both received and focused on reasons why, and what makes these people act in such a fashion. Remember when reading the stories that many have been collated prior to the Respect campaign and such tales prompted the FA to take action. They are a minority that at the time were destroying our game.

We begin with a worried and concerned parent in Yorkshire. Craig from Doncaster considers the coach responsible for what lead him to take his son out of a team. The team manager who was refereeing the game had lost it completely with the kids whilst they were playing. When he blew for half time Craig walked over to him and asked him to relax, (after all it was only a game and a friendly). The coach exploded in a storm of rage and started swearing at Craig, telling him to either take the whistle or keep quiet. Craig regrettably told him where to go and walked away. His son has never wanted to play for a team since.

The coach from this story was clearly stressed out, which could be due to the fact he was coaching and officiating at the same time. I've done it myself, after putting up the goals, the barrier, taken the warm up, organised the team and then the other team declines to help out with the officiating of the game. The solution is to speak with the team before hand about the situation and make sure somebody is available to do it. I officiated one of our teams in 2011 and received a lot of abuse from the opposition as the game was in their eyes "a top of the table clash". Now at the time of writing, the hostile visitors were Under 10 and they were unbeaten. The ball went out for a corner and I went with what I saw. The home team scored and the goal was met with great disharmony from the away side who decided (along with their parents) to verbally abuse me. The second half couldn't have got any worse for me, now the man in the middle, ready for a media grilling (for a decision that could have cost his team the title - give me strength!).

The ball bounced off me, hitting me on the thigh and into the path of one of our players. I knew the rule was to play on and remember seeing Howard Webb being involved in a similar incident in the Merseyside derby live on Sky Sports. Guess where the ball ended up? Yes, another goal for the home team who went onto to win the game. I felt guilty and sheepish but why? As a consequence of my apparent bad officiating I was barracked and made to feel a bad person. Their coach came over to apologise, and then in his next breath, began to criticise my so-called mistake as though he was Alan Hansen on the BBC sofa. Our parents kept their cool and in all honesty from that moment on, I knew I would write this book and research the problems more. I was sent messages of support and I was encouraged that a local FA official was present at the game to witness the whole sorry event.

Having visited tournaments in 2011 as a spectator, it is with little doubt that the disease is widespread. Teams from all over the north came together, only to be found at logger heads arguing on touchlines in an almost free for all. A male parent squared up nose to nose with a female parent; the caveman proclaimed *"You're just a set of cheating B*******'s!"* as the game went on with the players swearing at each other as passions rode high in the audience. The tournament organiser brushed the whole thing off and chose to ignore the incidents and let the show go on.

So going back to Craig's incident with the coach, there is no excuse to be aggressive when representing a club, particularly on a match day. Was the team manager provoked, or had he had a bad day, a hangover, a tough week at work, or an argument with the missus? He may have had money problems or a family illness. With all these things taken into consideration, should he have been out there in the first place? Or was he simply tired, or just had enough? Or worryingly was he the wrong person in the first place to be coaching Craig's son's team?

---

The Charter Standard FA check (now with an annual Health Check) ensures all the clubs have the correct people in place with the correct qualification and CRB checks.

*(CRB - Criminal Records Bureau. A government agency providing information on an individuals criminal record)*

When enrolling your child into a football club, ensure they have the Charter Standard mark and their health check is up to date. With this in place it gives the parent security that the club they are taking their child to a club who has everything in place and more importantly coaches with CRBs.

---

## Back to our stories...

Paul in Sheffield wrote:

"I'm all for encouraging kids to get into sport. My nephew plays for a local team, he's only six. They played a friendly match once where they were beaten by the visiting team. The coach of the visiting team, at the end of the match, got his team to bare their bums to my nephew's team! The coach of my nephew's team complained and was then threatened by the visiting coach. 1) Encouraging 6 year olds in this manner is inappropriate and 2) aggressive behaviour by the coach of the other team was out of order. Coaches should be role models to the young and easily encouraged and if this is what constitutes getting kids in to sport then I would rather my nephew didn't play. It all starts at the top in the Premier league where players are constantly swearing at the ref, badgering the ref and diving. My 6 year old nephew has certainly picked up the diving from watching Premier league football; hopefully he doesn't pick up some of the other traits!"

Paul from Croydon wrote on a forum that he feels it seems equally acceptable to hurl abuse at referees, coaches and the very young on the park, as it does on a Saturday afternoon at a professional match. He questions whether the same people would act the same at a tennis match or swimming gala? Unfortunately, the answer could sometimes be yes, as this style of "competitive dad"* will generally be the same, and probably miss his son or daughters Christmas concert on the grounds of "He's a queer and not competitive enough!" (*if you have seen the Fast Show with Paul Whitehouse, you will know exactly what I mean; check him out on You Tube!)

# THE DISRESPECT TIMES

## Parental aggression continues to blight youth football

Ian from the South West recalls how he saw a parent become increasingly frustrated with a 17 year old linesman and proceeded to project his anger onto the referee, threatening to "punch his lights out", if such calls were made again. Ian added that the referee on this occasion was his own son. Despite reporting the club to the league, Ian felt his son received no support or further help with this matter and he felt let down by the whole situation.

A coach in Brighton called Ben reflected that he has seen many punch-ups between parents at football over an under-9's game. Elsewhere on the south coast, a parent, Debbie, wrote that she had witnessed parents coming onto the pitch to punch a child because they have dared to tackle their child along with foul and abusive language from parents and other players.

A 12 year old in Salisbury reported being scared whenever his dad was linesman because of the amount of abuse he receives from the touchline. He is frightened, at what might one day happen to his Dad. He see's angry parents snarling at him if he puts his flag up. The boy also reported that if films had 18 year old restrictions for swearing then why was he subjected to hearing his father abused in such a way?

## The pushy parent in action....

Gary in Sheppy admits to being one of these pushy parents. He says his son's coaches do not like making substitutions, so unless you're one of his top boys, you simply don't get a look in. Gary lost his temper with the coach one day after he played a boy for five minutes, shouted and criticised him, then took him off. Then he did the same to Gary's son, but he timed him: four minutes he gave him, then told him he was no good. This is Under-8's football again! I have witnessed this first hand at this age group and have the role reversal going on within clubs, where members ask why we don't play to win or others who just simply want their kid to be the "top dog" every week; score; be man of the match; and have his mug shot in the paper. They don't really see the coach's job, which is to ensure all the players have the allotted playing time and leave with smiles, not frowns at the end. I've also witnessed parents sigh, moan or show their dismay when their potential 'Lionel Messi' is replaced by a beginner as their concept of equal opportunities theory goes out of the window.

David from Sidmouth asks is it a case of pushy parents or defending your player's skill? He speaks on behalf of any parent who has "lost it". "What would you do if your son was kicked and fouled regularly because he had a lot of skill?" he asks "Fouls not taken up by the referee and often not condemned by the parents". Now David's point is something that is worrying as he feels his boy is being targeted. I have heard skilful players being booed as they slot in goal after goal. How can you stop a boy scoring goal after goal if he's good enough? Make him pass? Make him have two touches? Surely this is hiding his natural talent. You only have to read any footballer's autobiography to hear them tell you how many goals they scored for school or their club. The one boy I remember that could literally score when his team needed to went on to become semi-professional. People used to moan he was too this or too that but like Dave says, it's a real difficult area. Though nowadays, if the skill is that high then the only real solution is to refer him to a local academy or school of excellence. I also know of a boy who was signed by a professional club, and allowed to play in tournaments for his club team. The result – whenever he played, he was man marked, kicked from pillar to post and had an array of bruises to show off. There is no wonder professional clubs protect their players even at a young age.

Phil from Romford admits that he once shouted abuse at a referee at his son's under-13 semi-final cup tie. Phil alleges that the ref could not be bothered to mark out the 12 yards for a penalty kick, and he would not take any notice of all the people shouting to him. The referee also did not know how long each half was due to last and instead of playing 35 minutes each half, he played 30 minutes and then 40 minutes in the 2nd half. Phil admits he was wrong in his actions and did apologise to his son's team mates and manager but he feels sometimes the games he watches are refereed by people who seem to have no understanding of the game or even the rules. Phil is typical of a frustrated parent and we now enter a vicious circle. The referee sounded like he needed support or was possibly not ready to be in the situation he was put in. Shouting abuse at him was not the answer and a more mature approach from those concerned may have solved the problems that occurred.

An alarming trend that can be seen when reading through people's experiences is the number of young players leaving the game because of the poisoned environment.

Robbie in Cheshire has three sons who played football but they all have packed up. The extreme and industrial language used by some parents and coaches and picked up by the kids, ruined it for him and his boys. The team his kids played for had a great coach and had good supporters but he found some of the opposition vile. The vast majority of parents just want to see their children having a good time and are very supportive of the efforts of the coach/manager, but as with most things in life, an unpleasant minority can spoil things for the majority.

Mr Palmer had to pull his son out of his football club. He felt there was so much pressure on his son and so much shouting from the sidelines from parents and the managers that it was beyond belief. His son used to leave training nights crying his eyes out as he was not picked for the weekend games. He had been told he was not good enough by the over zealous manager and this completely knocked his confidence. He was only 9 years old and just wants to play football and enjoy it. Mr Palmer's son knows he has skill and has since joined a new team and plays with a smile on his face. Parent, trainers and managers please take note...they are kids with delicate feelings!

Donna from Salford reports how her talented son was scouted several times but has now given up football at the under 11 age because of the abuse from the coach and parents. Another lady, Kim on the south coast, spoke of her son who was 16 years old when he stopped playing after being in the game since he was 6. He had reached a decent standard and went on tours with Portsmouth Football club. He constantly felt under pressure from managers and coaches to the point where football was no longer fun. The final straw came in a match where two of his team were taken to hospital (through reckless fouls) and the referee was intimidated by opposition parents. If police had been present there would have been grounds for assault charges. The opposition parents were verbally abusive, using language of the gutter, and became physically threatening to anyone who remonstrated with them. Six independent reports were sent off and no action was taken. Kim's son now plays rugby.

In 2003 Neil Botham's son, who was the goalkeeper for his local under 9's football team, conceded a last minute penalty to tie the game. As it was his eighth birthday that day, Neil was hoping his son may have a bit of luck and pull off the save, but it wasn't to be. Amazingly as the ref blew the final whistle for full time, the manager of the opposition ran 50 odd yards onto the pitch and slid on his knees in front of his son with his fists clenched in the pathetic footballers celebratory style, screaming "Get in there! We deserved that! You're not going to be top of the league much longer!" etc... Now Neil is not a violent sort of person and confronted the man, explaining to him that because of his actions his son would never play football again whilst people like him were allowed to be involved in the game. His son now plays rugby and has developed not only as a sportsman but as a person, far more than he ever would have done by being a footballer. As a cricket coach for juniors and also involved in the rugby scene, Neil now finds what goes on in football hard to believe!

Neil's son may never have been the next England goalkeeper, and he certainly won't be now, but his values in respecting referees and umpires in his sports transpose into everyday life. Neil says his son's people skills compared to his footballing class mates are second to none, as these kids often lack respect in other areas of life. Neil says he does not write this out of contempt for football but out of concern from a sport that, as a kid, he had so much pleasure from.

## Standing up for the parents...

One dad, Mark, feels that parents are an important part of any well run junior football club. He conceded that everyone can get over excited and but just want their child to be as successful as possible. He believes as long as the guidelines are set early on by the club and acted upon if not met, the situation can be controlled. Mark is involved with an U13 team and knows that emotions can run high and comments are made from the side of the pitch. However, he feels that as long as the comments are not directed at either one individual or the referee then we should be able to accept that. He concludes that encouragement for the team from parents is the best form of support. In my opinion, once comments from the side line start, events can quickly spiral out of control. I feel Marks comments are there to be shot at, so go ahead as Clint Eastwood would say, make my day!

## However, it's not all doom and gloom...

One season, Paul from Wycombe went to his son's team's first tournament. Before the first match all the parents were asked by the organiser for constructive support and encouragement. In particular, they asked all comments to be positive and to leave the 'tactics' to the teams' coaches. Paul's teams' parents were most impressed by this attitude and advice, which he would recommend for all junior games.

Andrew lives up north and his son plays for an under 9 team. He reported that luckily no incidents have happened so far when he has played. When his team go into games or tournaments, parents from both sides get on and compliment all players on both teams. He is shocked to hear what is going on around the country. He would like anybody to come over and watch when his team plays again so their club can show the rest of the country how to behave when we watch our kids play football. Parents wouldn't go on to the pitch if they were at Anfield, Old Trafford etc, so why should they when they are watching their kids play?

More positive reports like this need to be the focus within the media as we look to change this disease that is in the game. Though for every positive story, it seems we have at least ten negative ones...I found positive stories very hard to find.

## The view from a pro...

Gavin Strachan spent his early playing days with Coventry City and has played in the top four divisions and the Scottish Premier League. He also won 8 caps for Scotland Under 21's. Son of the more famous Gordon, he is a fully qualified UEFA B coach and runs a soccer school with his father and brother Craig. He wrote on his blog about some of the issues he had witnessed first hand in junior football. He was shocked when his little boy, aged only six at the time, was asked to go along to a centre of excellence session (obviously he can't name the club).

Even though Gavin was sceptical, his son wanted to go. They only went to two sessions. The parents were herded into a viewing room to watch the session. There were whole families in there watching these little kids. Some of them 'tutting' if they made a bad pass, comparing stories of the goals their kids had scored and what scouts had been to see them play. He could not believe the pressure that was being heaped on these children at the age of 6. He couldn't help thinking that if he was one of these lads and this much pressure was placed on him at such a tender age, he would have had enough of football by the time he had reached 11.

Does it matter how good the child is until he is 14 or 15? That is when clubs primarily make decisions on players. Until then they should simply have fun and try and learn the basics of the game in a non-pressurised environment.

You then have to ask the question: "What happens to the child if he does not make it?" I am sure, in most cases, the families are very understanding and soften the blow for the child, but what if they are not?

One of the coaches who works at a centre of excellence told Gavin of a meeting with a young lad, who was 14, and his Dad, at which the player was told he would not be kept on. Unbelievably the Dad turned on his son and said, "I told you, you were not working hard enough." Just what the poor lad needed!

Another interesting aspect of the forums and blogs is that it provides a voice for those being criticised within this book and gives an opportunity to see both sides of the story.

Other parents have told websites and forums more stories than this book could hold. I hope all these parents will one day visit a game and enjoy it in a safe friendly environment.

## 3. Referees and officials

In April 2009, the Cumberland Football Association admitted in the local News and Star that referees are throwing in the towel because they are fed up of having to put up with swearing, insults and threats in both junior and senior football. Cumberland FA chief Geoff Turrell came out and blasted Premier League stars for setting a bad example to children who copy those abusing referees. Turrell said:

"Apart from people getting too old, the main reason why we lose referees is because of the abuse they receive from the sidelines or from players. We lose around 20 referees a year and, when we ask them why, 70-80 per cent say they're fed up of the abuse. That's why they're packing up. We lose probably as many referees as we recruit every year. You only have to look at what happens on TV and if youngsters see Didier Drogba running up and abusing a referee, it's not a good example. I'm sure kids are influenced by it and they mimic them. It's really sad that some parents can't just let kids get on playing the game and, instead of interfering, let the coaches direct the youngsters on the pitch and allow the referees to get on refereeing the game. They are living their own lives through their kids. It's distracting for the kids and it's not allowing them to relax and enjoy the game."

The newspaper reported that on average, 7,000 referees quit football nationally every year because of the abuse they receive from players and from the sidelines. The FA had also revealed that many children also give up the game because of the attitude and actions of over-enthusiastic parents.

Regarding the introduction of the Respect campaign, Turrell said: "The campaign was undoubtedly overdue but it's going to be a marathon rather than a sprint because we won't change people's attitudes overnight."

As an experienced referee in Cumberland, 65-year-old Peter Crelling has been on the receiving end of sickening abuse from players, managers and spectators. Amongst Creilling's experiences was an occasion where he was forced to send off two players and award two penalties. One of the red-carded players stormed back onto the pitch and threatened him, forcing his team-mates to restrain him. Crelling said:

"There isn't much I haven't seen over the years. The last thing you want to do is abandon a game but I have been forced to do that, because things got so out of hand. I've been threatened by players but no one has actually hit me. I referee because I love it and I can handle the abuse. You get more respect from people than those who are hostile. Most of the unpleasant incidents tend to be isolated."

Crelling believes the Respect campaign should be more targeted at foul-mouthed Premier League players rather than grassroots level. He also believes that referees should adopt a more hard-line approach "If players see Premier League players getting away with bad behaviour, they think they can get away with it in the lower leagues as well. I was once running the line and informed the referee how I had been sworn at. He sent the lad off but other players questioned why, because they argued it happened all the time on Match of the Day. I have always been a hardliner, because I don't wish to hear foul and abusive language, especially if women and children are watching. I think some referees are too tolerant and they make a rod for their own back. I always get the two captains in the middle and tell them what I want and what I expect. I tell them to keep it clean."

Looking and reading many stories found again on the internet, it was obvious that plenty of referees had plenty of views and some worrying stories.

Anthony Burns in Staffordshire was the Referee in the final of a friendly (is there such thing?) tournament at Under 16 level. It was one of our rare hot summers and during the game he witnessed some disgraceful scenes between two parents. One parent of the losing team had initially kicked it all off and within minutes several others got involved and a mass brawl began between both sets of parents (supporters!?). Anthony was so shocked by what he was seeing that he abandoned the game in the interests of safety after consulting both managers and the tournament organiser. The organiser had probably put hours, days and weeks of work in: e-mails, posting invitations, phone calls, not to mention the setting up on the day - only to go home with this in his memory bank.

Anthony believes a solution would be the threat of banning any club whose supporters act this way from future competitions and tournaments. I back him and his ideas but for bigger clubs, this would mean heartache for other members. Once again, the minority ruin the fun for all involved. His other solution would be to sign an agreement before each match, stating that clubs are responsible for the conduct of their supporters and club officials. This could work. In my local league for instance, a card has to be sent with the result. Could the card become a bigger part of the match day with the Referee awarding a mark, along with both coaches, for conduct at the beginning and end of the game. More paperwork, more hassle I hear you cry, but nonetheless a useful proposal and idea from a referee who has witnessed something he would like address in our game. Or maybe this is already in use in some parts of the country?

Alan Hearn, a referee at Level 7 and qualified for 4 years, officiates league games at under 11 to 16 at his local club, and averages two games per Sunday. He tells of the worse incident he has ever seen, when a visiting supporter threatened to stab a club official who was simply running the line. Unfortunately Alan only found out at the end of the game, as if he had found out earlier, he would have taken action. He is adamant this type of behaviour comes from the TV, coupled with the total disregard shown by managers and TV pundits towards officials. It's a point that has been touched on many times throughout this book. Alan returns home every few weeks and looks to the sky and says "Why do I bother?", and many reading this will know that feeling and I certainly do. Though the message to Alan is that the game needs you, and we long to fight these awful situations.

Robert in Bristol is on the FA list of referees and is very proud of this. He feels it is wrong to send out new young referees to youth games to be verbally, or sometimes physically, abused. He is convinced that this is the reason for the falling numbers in youngsters wanting to referee. When this does happen, he would like a watching observer or official to help and make everyone aware of his presence. The observer would have the power to abandon a game if need be. This would work in theory and be a great idea, though, as he says, there is already a lack of referees. Would there be enough spare refs to help coach and educate the new refs? I'm sure in some FAs this type of situation operates. Our local young referee is always helped by us and educated. It's not a case of "Oh no! It's him!" like the feeling of being behind a learner driver!

In Essex a referee of 48 years and who is no longer involved in running a junior club, dedicates his time purely to officiating. He remembers a Cup Final when an Under 13 goalkeeper gave away a penalty for a foul. The 'keeper became very upset and the man in the middle explained to him that he would not caution him. However, the lad threw his gloves at him along with a barrage of abuse! He would not calm down and with this appeared the red card! The 'keeper then made things worse by kicking the goals and hoardings behind the goal. After the game the abuse continued, this time from the 'keeper's parents and spectators. One Mum shouted out that she hoped that the man in black got cancer and died a horrible death! Horrific and I really hope this lady is reading this, what a disgrace! Thankfully our referee in question is still running around pitches on a weekend and is fit and healthy. No doubt this Mum is still patrolling touchlines in Essex and hurling abuse at officials. The 'keeper, well what did he learn from the day? Not a great deal one would expect.

How could this have been managed better? I really wouldn't like to comment as I'm not a ref. It would have been easy to just ask the coach to sub the 'keeper but with this incident spiralling out of control, the ref had to stand his authority. The keeper saw red, and I assume the team lost. The mum went home and probably sank 12 cans of Stella to wash out her abusive mouth!

# THE DISRESPECT TIMES

## Parents hounding Referee's out of the game

Adam from Walsall, a referee on a Sunday morning, has a horrific story. He had an encounter with a parent who disagreed with one of his decisions, this ended up in an argument with Adam stating the laws of the game and pointing out that it is just a child's game of football. He was punched in the face in response as a consequence. Adam was just 16 years old!

Darren is only 14 and often referee's for a young team, even at away games, if the referee doesn't turn up. Darren is really dedicated but despite being only 14, still get threats from parents all the time.

Nicola from Devon quit refereeing children's football because of the problems with the parents. Frequently parents would be screaming abuse at their own child as well as others and on more than one occasion Nicola had to send parents away from the field because of their behaviour. Nicola had been threatened and verbally abused and all this in front of their own children.

A young referee was also abused on social networking sites after giving a penalty in a big game. The ref, who was a year older then the boys in the team, was subjected to vile and threatening messages. He was also bullied at school during that week, and came off the referee's register due to flack he had received. A very sad story indeed.

I hope by reading this, it is does not deter any young person entering the game to be an official. These are isolated incidents and the FA are doing their best to ensure that these problems are being dealt with by the leagues and clubs. Referees are hit hard, particularly in the media, and everyone I've ever known has given one grief at one time or another. At the highest level of the football, the future may see us bring in technology like that used in Cricket, Rugby and Tennis to help the professional referees. However, technology will never work in our local park, and I would pray that if it did come in, then it would help the grassroots referees in some way. If top officials use technology and grassroots don't, would this come into the parent's train of thought before they hurled obscenities at the often voluntary referee, that should at mini soccer be invisible and at youth football be there to control the game, and make decisions to help the flow.

I often cringe at the junior match reports I have researched whilst compiling this book, that in their words, the referee was awful and cost their team the game. The newspaper editor needs to look at who is writing this and then printing this. A dig at the official in the local rag will never help the matter as the writer copies the big tabloids and references what went on in the Super Sunday match at the weekend!

Andy is 17; he referees and also plays non-league football at a decent standard. He passed his course at 14, and has been lucky enough to officiate at the new Wembley. However, he frequently thinks about quitting as the teams really do not seem to understand that without refs there would be no game. Andy recalls one occasion were he gave a free kick which the team scored from. The opposition manager came on the pitch to threaten Andy repeatedly with violence and verbally abuse him; if he wasn't restrained by parents from the other team, Andy honestly believes he would have been attacked and subsequently left football as a referee. Andy truly believes it starts from the managers down, as after this guy had been restrained his team soon turned on him, with insults and gestures. Andy eventually had to abandon the game. Upon reporting this event to the league, no action was taken as they had "no evidence to suggest that this man's actions were unprovoked".

A story such as Andy's went by unnoticed, maybe because of his age, who knows, but the protection needed to be there for him.

The problem snowballs, these kids think it is perfectly acceptable to behave in that manner which brings on a whole other set of issues for the referee.

Sam used to referee youth football in Suffolk and at every game without exception there would be parents giving him and his colleagues verbal abuse. Every decision, irrespective of how clear cut, would be contested by the parents and this had a knock on effect to the children. He observed a change in attitude as he refereed different age groups - the older they get the more they argue decisions.

Joe is another 17 year old who has often thought of quitting. He learnt to take some of the minor abuse such as the odd swear word directed towards him but there had been much more extreme instances. Joe had taken control of an under 12s game and a team of parents and the coach (who was a mother) ganged up on him and shouted abuse throughout (it was a friendly and only his second game ever!). Their team was losing 5-0 and they had a shot cleared off the line. "The coach called me a disgrace and said it was the wrong decision" said Joe, despite her being on the half way line. Joe stopped the game, had a word with her and tried to explain his decision but she shouted at him and claimed Joe should have awarded the goal to boost her team's morale. She refused to shake his hand at the end which was very disheartening for Joe. There's morale and there is common sense, it looks like she was low in both.

Mark swapped from rugby league to the beautiful game to watch his son officiate and he was stunned. Having observed him referee some 40 games at U11 - U13, Mike said "it would seem that the source of most of the abuse towards the referee is the lack of knowledge of the laws of the game on behalf of the parents, and indeed sometimes the coaches. To address the loss of youngsters from the game, consideration should be given to not publishing the league tables and having promotions / relegations part way through the season. This would avoid teams having to struggle through a season being hammered 20-0 every week and would promote enjoyment of the game." All his thoughts have been put into the new proposals being forward by the FA in their Future Game project will surely help this situation and move teams from group to group if they are being beaten by double figures every week.

## The way forward...

The referee's stories are endless, but with no referee we will have no game. On April 11th 2011 Respect FC (featured with full details in section 5) asked for reports on vitriolic abuse, unacceptable criticism of match officials and players surrounding referees in an attempt to get opponents sanctioned. The right offences for Respect to target in the professional game

On their website they hold some great forums with views from all, and demonstrate how Respect can be introduced into the game by referees and club officials. The new guidelines are to be introduced ahead of season 2011-12, with new punishments.

PFA chairman Clarke Carlisle, a Burnley player at the time, said: "As long as the guidelines are clear we will support them. They need to make sure there are no grey areas so that referees can apply them consistently and players know where they stand."

Carlisle said the PFA's annual meetings with the Referees' Association had shown there had been a drop in the number of incidents involving players and claimed that when incidents did happen they were blown out of proportion. He added:

"The number of incidents where referees are accosted are becoming fewer and fewer. It is just that where incidents are highlighted they now receive massive, global attention. But the key is to make the guidelines clear because it can be a very emotive issue if it is subjective and incidents appear differently to different people. Respect has not failed at all.

The Referees' Association themselves have agreed the number of incidents - and the scale of the incidents - is reducing. It is definitely not failing but we are always looking to improve the image of the game"

Though the criteria for judging referees is; we look at their mistakes, we concentrate on them. These get magnified and blown out of proportion and the media, ever the propaganda machine, feeds on these errors and conducts media trials.

## Can they ever win?

Referees have long been the villains of the media and are scrutinised by managers to excuse a bad result and deflect pressure away from themselves.

In November 2009, a year on from the launch of the Respect Campaign, Mr Rooney was in the news again for all the wrong reasons.

After Manchester United were apparently robbed by the referee against Chelsea, Wayne Rooney walked off the pitch and mouthed "12 men" at the Sky Sports camera. He was warned by the FA over his future conduct.

Rooney explained his comments, acknowledging he probably shouldn't have said it but sure that he could have said worse!

"I was disappointed at the end of the game and felt we'd deserved more out of it," said Rooney. "Your emotions are high at the end. When I look back, I probably shouldn't have said it, although I maybe could have said worse! I felt we didn't get the decisions. But that's the way it goes. There have been games when we have got the decisions when we shouldn't have. As a team, it was probably the best performance we've had this season. It was a good performance but a disappointing result."

The following day a junior football team played away from home. After leading the game 4-1, they were pegged back to draw 4-4. The referee was 15, and at the conclusion of the game after a late penalty, the visiting skipper along with his parents mouthed "12 men" at the lonely official. The influence of the stars is here in black and white.

We see managers criticising referees before, during and after every game. We see players swearing at referees during games and complaining about them after games. This has to stop – the referees are part of the game, not a problem or threat to it.

## 4. The Player

The views I found from the young players were concerning to say the least. Many reported abuse that eventually stopped them playing the sport. Jack in London used to play for an under-13 team and suffered from immense nerves. It did not help him that his manager would shout and swear at Jack's team at any opportunity. Playing in an awkward position made Jack make many errors and the manager and parents would shout at him, making it a terrible experience overall. How can a child develop their football skills and have a good time if their manager and team's parents are shouting abuse at them?

I have witnessed it myself when a team were being "hammered" 6-0 (the coach's word as he berated the team trailing!). Little Johnny (here he is yet again) came on for team leading by six goals. His first touch was to give possession away and the other team subsequently scored. Poor Johnny was subjected to mimicking from his team mates, abuse from the sidelines regarding a clean sheet and was eventually re-substituted. Awful! The team went onto win 10-1. Little Johnny hardly got a kick; surely if he was deemed as being a weaker player then he should have had more allotted playing time in this game which was so one sided anyway. Though apparently not, according to the coach, who wasn't interested as his team needed goals, goals and more goals in case the league title went to goal difference. Oh my days!

Jonathan said in 2005, whilst playing for his local under 15's side, several of his team-mates and himself were racially abused by parents from the opposing team. They were called, 'monkeys' and told to, 'go back to the jungle'. The referee made no attempt intervene, but I'm not sure whether this was because he shared their views or felt intimated and feared for his safety should he object to the behaviour of the parents. Emile Heskey was subjected to this in Croatia playing for England in September 2008. Croatia later got a £150,000 fine. Maybe people only do these things due to what they hear and see and become arrogant that they won't get caught - much like a drink driver perhaps. A banana was thrown onto the pitch of an international friendly by a German student at Arsenal's Emirates stadium in 2011. The game between Scotland and Brazil recalled images of the 80s where a talented Watford side containing John Barnes were subjected to a weekly aerial threat of the yellow bendy shaped fruit.

Being racially abused is a whole new can of worms and opens a lot of debate and problems. The Kick It Out programme works tirelessly with this issue. While writing this I remember an incident that involved an Italian born player who was reported by a set a parents who had in fact abused *him* for 90 minutes. They reported that the player himself had been racist towards them and their players. The player in question was then brought in for a disciplinary hearing but thankfully cleared due to lack of evidence. Kick it Out have campaigns of their own and more information and how to sign your club up can be found on their website. www.kickitout.com

This next story is one that has been heard one too many times. A player of 12 years old left his local team (as the manager didn't play him) and joined another team in the same league. Later that season they played each other and former manager told each player when he got the ball to try and break his legs! The parents were shouting *"break his legs"*, *"cripple him"*, and other foul language. He was 12, and the Respect campaign surely has the force to stop this happening.

One parent ref sent an opposing player off for handball on the goal line. The game had to be stopped and the whole team refused to shake hands at the end. The parents abused the ref and stopped him from going into the changing rooms. The parents were acting like the kids and the kids are acting like the parents. A crazy situation and one we hope can be eradicated

Thankfully some players wrote they were still in the game after seeing incidents and many continue to play.

A 14 year old, Adam, was playing a friendly when he was fouled. It was a two-footed challenge from behind, after he had played the ball. The challenge was so reckless that Adam could not carry on playing. The referee was about to give the opposition player a card until all the opponents parents and supporters started shouting and harassing the official until he put the cards back in his pocket. Fifteen minutes later the same player punched one of Adam's team-mates and again the referee did nothing as he was simply bullied by the touchline.

Adam's coach later heard from another manager that the player who had thrown the punch repeated this act a few weeks later and had now thankfully been kicked out of the league. Could this have been prevented by earlier intervention? Possibly but it seems the parents won a battle with the man in black.

# THE DISRESPECT TIMES

## Young players leaving the game in droves

Martyn from Farnham saw his under-13 level manager punched in the face by the opposing team's manager mid-match. Needless to say this aggression then spread to the pitch. Almost every week there would an incident so Martyn reported that he had finally stopped playing, which is very sad to hear.

Thomas in London played in a game for his local team against the top team. The opposing parents were really aggressive and constantly shouting at the referee when he didn't give decisions their way. The manager was really aggressive and he fired up their players so much that even when they were winning 5-0 their captain threw a punch at one of their players and got himself sent off!
What a donut!

Andy gave up Junior Sunday league football 2 years ago because he could not handle the pressure. "If you performed badly in a match, the parents of your team mates would hassle the manager to sub you off" he reported. In a derby game, Andy's team were leading 5-0 after 50 minutes. The opposition rallied and pulled the score back to 5-5. Unfortunately, the match never reached its conclusion - the game had to be abandoned because the parents of both teams started fighting!

One player remembers a match when a parent openly criticised not only the referee, but also his son's team and manager. Whenever his son received the ball he would bark commands at him, often the opposite of what the manager would say. If he was tackled or didn't do as he was told, then a barrage of insults would follow, using language that was an absolute disgrace, certainly for an adult to be using to a child of 14.The parents also heavily criticised the referee, and on several occasions openly criticised the manager who refused to respond to the outlandish comments. When the game had finished (their team lost 4-0) the parent refused to look at their child and again confronted the referee with an onslaught of abuse, the player had never seen anything quite like it. Parents like this need to be reminded that Sunday league football is purely about enjoyment and these people suck the fun out of football.

Paul is somebody with strong opinions and has played in junior Sunday Leagues for a number of years. He feels the referee's are as much to blame as the parents. He felt the bad decisions from the refs are the trigger for parents to start shouting and arguing. (I don't share his views here - there is no excuse!)

He feels competition is too high in Sunday league. At academies, the aim is to develop players and only the coaches can speak to the players but in Sunday league a small minority of managers and parents just want a win for their team at all costs and they are able to voice their feelings. He went on to say he has played in games where his team mates have all been keen to get on with the game while referee's coaches, and parents stand there arguing.

# THE DISRESPECT TIMES

## Young players continue to quit in disgust

John played at under 16 level. He described a match where coach of the opposing team had to officiate due to the appointed referee not turning up. About 60 minutes into the match, his team were leading 2-1 and the opposition were getting very frustrated. One of John's team mates made a poor challenge and the coach-cum-referee became very aggressive. John's captain stepped in to try and calm the situation down and irrespective of the fact he was the referee and an adult he started a fight with the skipper (a child by law) and head butted him full in the face causing a fracas. The game was then abandoned.

Tom thinks red cards for parents is a great idea and wants it to come into use. Would it be respected though?

Chris plays under 14s football and had one game stopped because the referee was the same age as the players and he was simply overwhelmed by parents, players and coaches so much so it was abandoned!

One player quit after his coach told him he could only play against the weaker teams in a tournament. He even said he could captain his second string 11, and likened it to a Carling Cup team. A Carling Cup team is what the top Premier League put out, to rest their key players. It must be a blow to a young lads self –esteem to be told that.

## Fortunately, it's not bad news all the way...

Daniel played for Burton Albion U13s and proclaimed they have no problem of abusive parents as their league states that it will not be tolerated, although Dan does worry that the managers are more of a problem.

James finished playing junior football in 2008 and declared he loved it and didn't have much trouble from parents off the field at all. The main reason being for this was because James's team had an ex-professional as the manager. Most parents respected him and knew that he knew best for the team and for the players and James feels it would be a great idea for ex-players to give back to the community and get involved in grassroots football. A lot of ex pros are involved with academies and with youth teams through the leagues, though it wouldn't hurt for more to be involved at club level. At our club, the club captain of ex-league club Scarborough (now Athletic) runs one of our teams, and the respect is instant.

An under 11 keeper who had been shipping double figures all season mentioned to our goalkeeping coach (ex-Bridlington Town Keeper Nick Tudor) that he loved it , as he had plenty of action and if he was in a top team he'd get bored with nothing to do. Nick was pleasantly surprised and this just shows that the kids don't really care about the score and results.

A fascinating story comes from Paul, who at 15 years old, behaved more like a mature adult and leader than any of the watching parents in a semi-final cup game. The parents and managers of both teams were giving all the players hell. About five minutes into the second half, the referee blew his whistle and stopped play as two parents (one of which was Paul's dad!) had started fighting. As captain, Paul walked over to the other team captain and asked him what he would think about all the players on both teams walking off the pitch. So to the amazement of the feral, frenzied adults on the touchline, both teams walked off the field of play. The match was abandoned due to their actions and Paul didn't speak to his embarrassing Dad for a week afterwards. The game was eventually replayed and Paul's team were defeated two goals to one, though the game was played in a different atmosphere to the first match.

The player is the most important person in junior football, and if they aren't enjoying it, then what is the point!? "Its kids football" and it is said a million times every weekend, though the prizes on offer can sometimes cause the problems we read. The player has to enjoy the football and play with a freedom to express themselves with no pressure from anyone.

There are some fantastic players out there, who share pitches with players of different abilities, gender and age. Some play for fun, some play to make friends and some play to be fit and healthy. There isn't a player in the country at junior football level that will play to be shouted at or simply embarrassed by somebody else. Ask your child why they play football!?

Recent research by the FA highlighted the fact that children played for no more than fun and to make new friends. Winning was almost bottom of the pile. It is difficult to compare the winning, with competing and developing.

Life is a competition from the minute you are born as we compete for relationships, we compete for affections, we compete for places at education establishments, we compete for employment etc, etc, etc, sometimes we are disappointed and that's part of growing up and learning about life. Football is no different. Schools have tried the "non competitive" tack in sports activities but they have now found that attitudes towards learning have been affected by this approach i.e. if you don't have to try your hardest to win – you don't need to try your hardest to learn. School sports have now retracted and installed winners and losers. It's a tough area to separate.

I am all for trying anything new if it helps develop the kids but no matter what we change, the main thing in my eyes that needs to happen is the time of year the fixtures are played. As has been highlighted by many coaches, the amount of fixtures that fall by the wayside due to bad weather is ridiculous and the fact that at the young ages the fixtures are not rescheduled due to the fact they are not competitive games means that kids miss out on a lot of football. Also playing in the winter months can put the kids off playing.

The idea of playing in the summer months will have its critics, as some kids play cricket and tennis also. There are tournaments available, and occasionally the weather can be too hot, with hard dusty pitches. Mini Soccer's future could lie in the summer months. Watch this space.

## 5. The Onlooker

The following stories were written on forums and are the most worrying of all the groups in this section. The onlooker may not even know what football is all about yet and stand as a witness to the problems that have been happening all over the country. Onlookers could be anyone: a passer-by or dog walker; an FA official; or even a local scout of a big club. What does this show those people? How does it really reflect on our game? The onlooker is the person that maybe watching due to the fact that they don't want to be involved or may be looking to get involved. I always worry about the onlooker, the person that arrives at the side of the pitch, and I'm not aware of who they are. I'm wary of these people, whether they are the random Grandparent or the local FA rep. This is why it is important that the Code of Conduct is implemented at all times to all family members that watch.

Jason is now just an observer by choice. He used to work at a County FA and they introduced an innovative scheme in the late 90s where teams had to rope off the playing area. There was a sign saying "cross this line and get a fine" and it stopped parents from trying to come on to the pitch. Jason reckons he could write a book on bad parents at football matches from his experiences – Looks like I beat him to it! He hasn't refereed for five years now. Over the years, he has witnessed managers fighting and fans fighting including one game where a team set fire to the changing room after losing! He concluded that he was glad he was no longer involved in the game due to what he had seen.

Dan is happy about the fact something has finally been done about kids playing on big pitches but why did it have to be initiated after our 'I'm a celebrity' national team (i.e. England) failed to make an impression in the 2010 World Cup. Dan is adamant the problem has been growing for years and organisations like Give us back Our

Game and Don't X The Line are a credit to society. There are Dad's and coaches like Paul Cooper and Mal Lee around the country that have to be a key part of how this country reinvents its grass roots game. Paul and Mal's campaigns are featured in section 5.

# THE DISRESPECT TIMES

## Onlookers amazed by sights on local park

Bob lives in Aylesbury and lives close to a park where kids'
games are often playing football right outside his window.
Bob reported that the language is usually awful from the
parents, and the aggressive tone in their voices doesn't help
anyone!

In Cardiff, Luke wrote that one Saturday, there was a game
which was being played on the park behind his house, and
just before work he decided he would go and watch a bit of
the game, though on his arrival there was a brawl erupting
between two parents from the same team!

Sam knows a boy who plays in goal and if he lets in a goal
his dad screams and moans at him and he gets upset. The
boy is only 7 years old!

Richard believes that most people have forgotten that it is
just a game, and they should not be trying to mould the next
David Beckham!

If a kid has the special something then it will show naturally.
More often than not kids in this country that play football
will end up playing for fun anyway. Richard says "Just face
the facts, and stop scaring and bullying our kids!"

Ian, another onlooking contributor, thinks nothing will improve until the top players learn to show respect for officials. They are the children's heroes and they set the trends. Learning from rugby union and having a 10 minute sin bin for dissent or inappropriate behaviour could work. Also, only let captains talk to referee (which is part of the Respect campaign). This will eventually create a culture where referees are respected and admired. Rugby players, coaches and followers of the sport have long looked at our sport and wondered why there are so many problems.

Another spectator, Joe, believes the theory that there is no friendly football game unless you let the young kids play on their own terms. The kind of pressure adults bring is not always welcome. Football is a game that is played for enjoyment but the kids also want to win, so you have to strike a balance where parents should encourage their children to enjoy playing football and let the coaches introduce the relevant competitiveness gradually.

Many of the comments on the forums confirm the theory that compiling league tables for mini-soccer has a negative impact. Kids are put under immense pressure by adults to win 3 points; they have little freedom to experiment and develop skills and techniques; they are unable to develop decision making skills because of the constant instructions of "get back, go forward, shoot" etc. Many children are rejected at a very young age because leagues only allow a certain number of players leading to selection processes; kids stand around in the cold as subs and coaches throw clip boards to the floor in frustration because the pursuit of 3 points is top priority. I firmly support the Give Us Back Our Game campaign which promotes child development, no subs and encourages adults to facilitate the kind of football experiences which allow our children to "fall in love with the beautiful game". In my experience, Little Johnny comes off the pitch happier if he's played well; maybe back-heeled a pass, tried a Cruyff turn or taken a good throw-in but lost the game, than if he stayed at the back, passed a few times and his team has won 12-0. Let's encourage our children to play football, NOT to win 3 points!

## More views from the sidelines...

Fred lives opposite an area containing at least 8 pitches for all ages. From Saturday morning until Sunday afternoon sitting in his garden is not an option as the language is terrible, and this is from supporters and players of all ages. Adding to his frustration is the amount of litter left. In his opinion the councils who rent out the pitches should monitor the situation and if necessary fine the clubs involved. Now Fred could be similar to an old lady close to my heart who simply hated kids. She once came out with a bucket of water as she believed that the school field should be kept quiet at the weekend. Though it beggars belief that people buy houses near schools and football pitches but do not want to hear the sound of sport on a weekend! However, Fred could be hearing a sound akin to a nightclub filtering out at 5am and if this is the case, then those who were on show that day should hang their head in shame.

Wayne has been a football fan for over 20 years, and supports Tottenham Hotspur with his two sons, who one day he hopes will play the nations favourite game. Though Wayne worries because they sit and watch football with him and what they see and hear completely puts them off. It would be shame if Wayne's kids aren't playing don't you think?

Charlie is also of the opinion that there is too much pressure on kids to perform due the fact they play competitive football too young. Children should be encouraged to develop, to copy the positive parts of football - the tricks, the passing and not the "win at all costs". It can be a form of abuse when young children are shouted at by parents and coaches. Children's confidence is seriously impacted and he is not surprised that Britain has the highest dropout rate in Europe. The Government must act before this goes too far. Only 1 in 1000 will make it to professional level according to some reports. Parents must get off the kids back and let them enjoy football. Yes, encourage them to win, but it's not everything. I fully agree with Charlie's opinions and another contributor, Chris, speculates about the root cause of the pressure: "parents who are gobby and offensive are generally either failed footballers or pushy parents with pound signs in their eyes. The only way to stamp this behaviour out is to ban the parents from the games completely. If you want to watch, get qualified and help out your local club. It's a game, get real."

Colin applauds the Respect campaign's efforts to clean up grass roots football but still thinks more action is required at the top level. He believes the media do not help because of frequent accusations that a referee is "spoiling the game" by merely upholding the laws of the game. He acknowledges that TV pundits are paid to be contentious but asks how often during a game do we need to hear 'that would have been a booking if he had not already been booked the referee showed good judgement in not spoiling the spectacle'. In Colin's opinion the referee shows appalling judgement in those circumstances. If a booking is justified it should be levied and if this means we have some games finishing 8 aside so be it. An interesting point.

Neil says that he thinks a lot more should be done to raise awareness of the parents and coaches. Perhaps modules in the coaching courses should be devoted to the power of psychology, rather than how to teach certain skills. Neil's ideas are great, and I feel parents should have to undergo a course, or at least an induction, before they sign up their child. The FA do have these courses in place, and a parent certificate can be found on the FA website.

He went onto say that during games, a lot of parents might think they are encouraging their children or helping them out. As a coach, I like to watch players react from making mistakes not being berated from family members for making them. Neil coaches swimming and always gives positive feedback to the things children do right rather than negative feedback to the things they do wrong. This goes much further in the development of a child.

To help parents notice this, coaches and parents need to work together on the side line to give more positive feedback. If parent wants the best for their child and wants them to go as far as they can in football, then this approach has to be taken.

Manchester City began a policy in 2011 where they asked for silence on their youth academy touchlines. Even from the coaches, which they feel parents will find strange. City expect to have some critics, and I'd like to go along one day and see it in action. The players will be asked to learn by their mistakes. Ok, we are not all Manchester City, though the example is set by one of the so called "Big Teams".

# THE DISRESPECT TIMES

## Onlookers aghast at parental behaviour

Alex lives in Peterborough and thinks the abuse from touchline is unbelievable. He went to watch his brother play and two women were shouting at each other across the pitch having a slanging match like those seen on Jeremy Kyle most week day mornings. How nice is that for the kids? After the match they even started fighting outside the changing rooms. Alex commented he wouldn't be going back to watch his brother play, and this leaves a sour taste in his mouth.

Sarah often goes to see her boyfriend's little cousin play in his 5-a-side tournaments, and the amount of parents there who become aggressive is scary. She's witnessed them cursing and swearing at members of the opposite team, and even seen parents encouraging their children to be violent. We're talking about ten-year-olds here! At the end of one match, a young boy walked off in tears because the opposing team and their parents had shouted obscenities about his mother

One onlooker told a story of a parent coach whose eldest boy played in another team at the same club. He overheard in his local gym, that due to his eldest not starting the game, he went to the match to start a fight with the coach. The coach had not started him as the previous week he had not turned up, without an excuse. The coach quit due to the fathers reaction, and vowed not to return.

Under Pressure
Queen and David Bowie 1981

## Coaches

Team managers and coaches are responsible for their own behaviour, along with that of their players AND of supporters. After each game the manager completes a match card which is sent to League officials. There are occasions where complaints have been raised about other clubs but NO follow-up action has been taken by the relevant League other than to feature in the next month's newsletter, repeated month after month to the point of boredom. Respective League (and County FA) officials need to attend more games and ensure that Managers are fulfilling their responsibilities that they take on. That is the feeling of all the coaches I researched on several websites that provide information for those involved all over the country.

I remember when I began coaching when it was very difficult to gain any resources though over a period of time I have built up my own workshop. Today, with the use of the internet, session plans, books and DVDs; more resources are available, making life easier for the coach if they can translate the information they are provided with. Some may use it constructively, though some use it as another reason to get highly flammable before a game.

## Do you want a happy, successful team?

You won't get all your decisions right all the time and neither will the referee. You are the gaffer, the boss, the coach, the manger or whatever else you or people call you and the team will follow your example. If you rant and rave, so will they! How many of us ever got better at something in response to someone swearing or throwing tea cups at them? There is something sad and quite alarming to see grown adults shout at children because they concede a goal or make a mistake.

The voluntary coach is by far the hardest job in junior football and one that comes under a huge amount of criticism. We can all be the England manager after a defeat, why did he do this and why did he do that? Likewise at grassroots the same questions are asked of the coach, who is sometimes a busy parent.

The coach is put in a precarious position and is always open to criticism. Stories emerge of coaches quitting due the pressure of the position. I said earlier that technology has helped coaches in some ways but it has also created problems unimaginable a few years ago. I was once told of a coach, also a teacher, whose team was in fact top of the league. But this didn't make him immune to cyber-bullying. His Under 13 group of boys began by abusing the coach, via social networking sites, for a minor incident that occurred in training. They also believed his assistant was more knowledgeable than him and began to try and oust the coach on Facebook. The coach was totally unaware of the situation as he did not use Facebook. He was made aware by a concerned parent. Despite the team being promoted, the team was folded due to 3 of the boys and the assistant's antics on the social networking site, with the assistant ganging up on the coach as he wanted the position of Head Coach so badly. A sorry tale which must have been stressful for a man who had given up his time to coach the children. I hope the assistant coach recognises his mistake and will in the future spend his time more productively than chatting to twelve year old boys on Facebook.

Matthew Simmons, the allegedly racist supporter who was on the wrong end of Eric Cantona's infamous kung-fu kick in 1995, was found guilty in 2011 of assaulting his son's football coach in south-east London. Fortunately that level of violence is rare. But an atmosphere of aggression and intimidation is all too common towards coaches.

Give some people a football pitch and their own team, with their own kid in it and on occasions they can lose it. Something takes over them like a man possessed.

The stories are quite alarming and most people I've chatted with on the subject of the coach agree that if the boss is howling abuse, then the parent's then players will follow. It starts at the top.

One finding from a forum in Sheffield (along with the response), gives us all food for thought:

"Kids need a good rollicking if they aren't pulling their weight and helping out their team-mates, makes them learn valuable lessons for later life that slouching and laziness is unacceptable. The same as in a classroom. So long as its words and not fists that are thrown, I can't see a problem."

The response…

"I think most people would rather have a slap than a tirade of demeaning words and being humiliated and abused by either their father or a coach, whether in front of a crowd or in private. It's the most demotivating thing that anyone can do to anyone.
Hurtful words to a child can stick with them for a lifetime."

Worrying words from two people who feel this strongly. Neither is a solution and only letting players learn from their own mistakes can be the real answer. We all get frustrated from time to time, but must take time to let the players learn without being howled at. I'm very vocal when I coach but only giving positive feedback and encouragement throughout the training or game. A positive negative, is much more worthy than a negative, negative!

The late, great Alex Stock, manager of QPR & Fulham got it spot on when he said about the modern youth game:

"Everywhere I go there are coaches telling young boys not to do this and that and generally scaring the life out of the poor little devils. Junior clubs playing with sweepers and one and a half men up front, no wingers, four across the middle. They are frightened to death of losing, even at their tender age, and it makes me cry."

Paul Cooper from Give Us Back The Game wrote an article for the Footy 4 Kids website who often provide good information with resources and a free newsletter rounding up information and feedback from those in the game.
He said bewilderingly:

"I once watched an under 9s game where one team had the coach and assistant coach standing by each goalpost continually barking orders to the keeper. Meanwhile, a parent on each touchline ran up and down shouting other instructions. When they won a corner at the other end their coach hollered "Wait" and trundled the entire length of the field for a minute's discussion, cupped hand in the ear of the poor flustered corner-taker who knocked his corner kick straight out.

The next game I saw was an under 8s. The team came out for a 30 minute warm-up which would have exhausted a crack team of US Navy Seals, involving running around the pitch, shuttle runs, sit ups and press ups with not a ball in sight. The substitutes weren't used as, according to the coach, the game was too close, and the kids were all kept in the changing room for 30 minutes after the game for a debrief. (The coaches had their initials sewn onto the front of their tracksuits. One was WR and the other ST. Use your imagination as to the missing letters.)"

I am sure he is not alone in the things he has witnessed and I have seen and heard more stories similar. From sleepless nights ahead of big Under 11 games to coaches going to the extreme lengths of cheating to win a football match.

My wandering around the Grassroots show in June 2011 show led me to stumble across Robbie Savage who conducted a seminar about Coaches being the role model.

He asked the question if anyone in the room would simply cheat to win a game. Half the room raised their hands. Half the room, I take it full of parents, players and coaches. I abruptly left, nothing against Robbie, but more in shock that half the audience felt that way.

One posting on Footy 4 kids forum, explained how the problem with the coach can grow as the team progresses and gets older.

**"Sorry to sound cynical, but how many U6 teams start off like the excellent example and end up with the horror stories creeping in as they reach 9 or 10 and older? That was exactly like my son's old team - fun for all from age 5 to 8, the then coach got more shouty at age 9, after that - equal playing time went out of the window, one sub was not played at all and in one game, parents of the stronger kids starting putting pressure on not to play some players at all, to holding trials at age 11, and punch ups on the pitch at 12."**

Even coaches who start out with the best intentions are under enormous pressure to start treating the kids like adults by the time they are 12. Those who try to resist are often hounded out.

I've often thought how difficult it would be to take a team from Under 7 right through to Under 18. Would a school teacher be expected to teach them to read and write then put them through their GCSE's and beyond? I'm sure most would argue that this is the norm and continuity for the players and some managers and coaches can lead to success. On the flipside, if there are problems with players, parents or the coach, the problems can easily rumble on. I guess the real fact of the matter is that the coach is usually one of the player's parents and has to move through the years with the team. At our club we followed many academies philosophy and that used at Manchester United where the coach remains at the same age group each year and the team moves up through mini soccer. Once the team reaches youth football, we look to develop both team and coach and they work hand in hand through the latter stages of the team's career.

Co-founder of the 'Give Us Back Our Game' project, Rick Finoglio, campaigned to put fun back into football and encouragement amongst youngsters.

## Ban Parents!

He proclaimed that "Too many coaches don't know what they are doing, and are just screaming on the side lines" Manchester United saw his changes and quickly incorporated them. His changes were to play 4 a-side and parents were not allowed anywhere near them with the kids even officiating the games.

Rick added "You would be amazed at how disciplined and organised they become. They get time on the ball and above all learn more skills"

Our younger brigade will try this out and we are also looking at bringing our older players in to assist with their training and officiating of the games. The hope is that they can be involved in making the change.

The job of coach remains, quite simply, the toughest task in junior football and those that undertake the voluntary position have to appease everyone involved from the club officials to the players then the parents who sometimes moan and groan at every decision.

The position can be enjoyable, winning trophies or having a successful team; though it can be a horrible experience as despite your efforts your team sit at the foot of every league and concede goal after goal, and your so called best player engineers a move with the help of his father to the team at the top.

The call for no league tables can help resolve these problems though there will always be one team crushing another by double figures every Sunday somewhere in the country.

When coaches are threatened, bullied or led to do things they regret, the role has to be looked at as not enjoyable.

Through all the stories of the coach I have trawled, the pressure that is put on the leader can be crucial to how he/she performs the role. To win the league, 3 points, score a goal, provide equal playing time for each player, to make all the parents happy and all this whilst having some kind of enjoyment themselves from the game. Without that pressure from those above and around, the position can be more relaxing and both coach and players can learn from football.

There are also, as always, many positive stories on the forums and the Respect campaign has indeed brought people and clubs closer together. From pennant exchanging, to helping with the matchday preparations, coaches can work together and not just be seen as in direct opposition. Having a laugh and joke on the sideline can break the ice between the two teams, and with the barriers on one side allowing the parents to mingle, it has helped the coaches to mingle. A far cry from the old school version where it looked more like a scene from Braveheart, as they stand every man, woman and child opposite each other, blazed in club colours as if poised to charge at each other once the whistle blows.

Children play football for enjoyment and the majority of the reasons they participate in sport are intrinsic. The top priorities are:

- To learn and improve their skills
- To have fun
- To be with friends
- To experience the excitement of competition
- To enhance their physical fitness
- To demonstrate their competence

Notice that the extrinsic goal of winning and beating others is not at the top of the list.

Coaches need to instill that into their armoury for the every day game. There are times and places to win at all costs, as Paul Ince reiterated earlier in Part 1 but junior football isn't do or die, with jobs on the line.

The coach will always be scrutinised, good or bad. They are there to be shot at by the parents. They have to go through so many rigorous procedures to get where they, yet are to be blasted by all and sundry. Praise is welcome for the coach, as well as the children. Not in a big-headed way, just for when an improvement is seen. The role is voluntary and can take over people's lives.

Help is needed from all members of the club to develop the coach, whether for extra courses or on match days, with the warm up or putting the goals up. Clubs must club together and we often witness this all round the country every Sunday. The finger is only pointed at a few, though it is that few that are being put under torturous pressure every week.

The following pages reflect on how coaches have felt negative and positive:

# THE DISRESPECT TIMES

## LETTERS PAGE

I have worked at an academy for one of the top clubs in the Premiership. The way that some parents hurl abuse at their children for making a mistake during a game is despicable. One cannot help but feel sorry for the children concerned who are under such immense pressure to perform, with not only influential coaches, but their pressurising parents watching. The majority of parents simply stay quiet and enjoy the game, occasionally cheering their children on, but there are always those, usually fathers, who feel they need to embarrass their children to make them play better. Sadly, the only way forward is to ban all parents from watching under-16's play.

*Neil in London*

I run an under-14 team but the parent pressure is fever pitch. I even had a parent ring me from the other side of the pitch demanding his son be brought on. In my experience some of the fathers put so much pressure on their children that it adversely affects their game! The constant instructions shouted by parents mean that the poor kids do not play their own game.

*Jas, Seven Kings*

I'm an Under-9's football coach and manager so I always see different situations with young players and their pushy parents who try to encourage but basically just bully their kids. They don't leave it to the coaches and let the child enjoy themselves. A child will lose their love for the game and fall away from football and football could lose a possible great player of the game.

*John W, Sunderland*

## LETTERS PAGE cont...

When I was asked to run a boys' team (I also ran a girls' team) I was very naive and thought the object was fun. When teams came to our pitch I would introduce myself and the players. I soon discovered that such acts of friendship were wasted. Most teams reflect the coaches and manager. I trained my teams to play football, and we did win things. But many of our opponents and parents would try and create an intimidating environment and cheer when a nasty challenge was made.

Referees are generally weak and, so, tackles get out of hand. Some managers have visions of being like Ferguson or Wenger and are 'empire' building on the backs of the children. I would train a child of any standard, but a lot of teams 'cherry pick' players in an attempt to win at all costs. Dreams of their child playing for England blind them to reality and all the child remembers are screaming parents, aggressive opponents and mad coaches. My teams will remember laughs, loyalty and playing the beautiful game.
*Dave, York*

## But there is hope! Here are some more positive stories...

Geoff says...
I am involved with a team in the Bolton & Bury District Junior league and from my experiences this is a superbly run league with over 4,500 children playing every week. The number of incidents of abuse to refs, bad behaviour are few and far between and certainly considerably less that you see in the Premiership these days. The children in the League are taught respect for the other team and to accept victory and defeat with good grace. Maybe we have been lucky to find such a well run league but I really don't see the same massive issues outlined on a regular basis.

Kevin says...
I'm currently managing an under 13 team in the Sheffield Junior Sunday League. We are a charter standard club and I am currently a level 1 coach toying with the idea of taking level 2 (if I can find time). Having taken the same team through from under 8's to under 13's I can fully appreciate the issues raised on Sky Sports. I have also refereed many junior games so I know what it can be like on the receiving end of disgruntled parents. Just recently I witnessed something that totally epitomised what Junior football is or should be all about. One Sunday when we had no fixture I went to watch some of the other games taking place at our club. I was watching a mini soccer game where mixed sides were playing independently having a great time, surely this is what Junior football is all about for the young ones .I must admit I've never really witnessed abuse to a qualified ref in junior soccer only to coaches doing their best.

Positive stories continued…

Ian says…

I'm taking on a young team starting next season for a well established youth club. I plan on not only educating children but to also educate the parents of these children as to what I expect from them. I understand peoples winning attitude but football is about taking part. Numerous parents want their child to be the next Ronaldo but we all know this isn't always realistic. Children are there and should enjoy the game…. that's all children not necessarily the more talented ones. Whilst children need guidance with football… the parents need educating in what their children really want…. taking part.. enjoyment….this is why I feel the need to work in this environment…

Another Ian says…

I am a manager of an FA chartered club. I am a level 1 coach (which all our managers have to be). Our club has a strict code of conduct and it is very well adhered too. Not all parents set bad examples as people seem to think. The parents of my team are very well behaved and realise that any hassle they cause looks bad on them, me and the players and severe indiscretions will result in expulsion from the club. Having said that we all want to win and it is a competitive and emotive sport. The players want to win, and the parents want to see them win and it doesn't always happen. We just have to learn to deal with defeat as well as success. I have been involved in mini soccer and 11 a side and been involved as a player all my life. I have witnessed just about everything positive and negative with adult football so probably I am a little hard nosed to any abuse thrown from opposition.

I am a big supporter of junior referees and basically just grateful that they are there to referee my games. I will not tolerate any abuse to referees. I've refereed games before and made a complete hash of it so I know just how difficult it can be without verbal abuse from the touchline. Of course they do make mistakes but who doesn't and its how you as a manager deal with those decisions that set the example to players and supporters alike.

## Aboard

With my experiences abroad, I felt it was only fair to end this section with a view from overseas. With the FA looking at the different systems used across Europe and the success of Spain and Germany in recent times, a lot can be learned from our counter parts. Jamie Jackson from the Guardian reflected in April 2011 about the football model in Holland. He noted that in the Netherlands, the overall philosophy is to always focus on ball possession to create opportunities. They also had little, if any, parental presence on the touchlines, with the sound of the boys and girls boots against the turf, and the movement of the rolling football being the only sound you can hear following instructions from their qualified coach. In Spain, who currently dominate world football, they focus on ball retention from an early age.

"If we want our kids to be like Messi, stop forcing them to play on full-sized pitches with screaming mums and dads on sidelines"
Shaun Custis – The Sun June 27th 2011

## A view from Cyprus...

Carolos Tikita, from Nicosia in Cyprus is a youth coach (Under-12 and Under-15) and coaches at an academy in Cyprus. Carolos found most parents come along to cheer and support their kids but any negative behaviour can affect the kids. He gets dirty looks in training if any 50/50 decisions are awarded to the other team (even though the "other" team is comprised of team mates). He agrees wholeheartedly that the game should be more enjoyable than competitive at young ages. The right mentality starts at home, so as parents and coaches our responsibility is clear. To have parents remonstrating decisions at training sessions is something that is clearly a problem.

## Disrespect in Sweden...

Jim Laursen from Skellefteå in Sweden (ex UK) was a coach for a team of girls and he witnessed young children being pushed through three or four training sessions a week in winter, then two or three matches in the summer. It was when he switched to being a referee that things really came to light for Jim. Too many parents on the touchline were abusive and disrespectful of the game, its rules, the officials and ultimately the teams playing.

"A parent who thinks their child is the next Pelé also thinks we should all be Phil Scolari coaching or Per-Luigi Collina officiating" expressed Jim. The treatment he received both during and after one game was enough to force him to quit refereeing completely and quit the club he was coaching. What Jim witnessed in Sweden was identical to the problems that had been occurring in our country.

The Swedish press reported that parents had to be separated by police at a youth game as several players looked on in tears. Swedish news website The Local reported fighting broke out in the stands during a semi-final match of the Alliansen indoor soccer tournament at which 12-year-old boys were competing. "I've been a coach for many years, and it's the worst thing I've ever seen," Mans Ahlm, the trainer for the Asums BK youth soccer club, told The Local.

What sparked the disturbance, which involved parents kicking and punching each other, remained unclear, but as many as 35 people were involved at the height of the incident .Four police cars arrived to calm things down, but no arrests were made. Witnesses said the incident was traumatic for many of the boys, with some reduced to tears. The teams were set to play again in the tournament's final round but both coaches agreed not to play the boys whose parents apparently sparked the fight, in a bid to avoid another incident.

## In Belgium...

Walter Zelta is a referee in Belgium and he says the problem is also an issue in his country. In Belgium there is a safety zone away from the pitch where only players and officials are allowed. There has to be a physical barrier around every pitch as if the safety zone isn't there then there is no match!

Abuse in youth games is a problem and mostly because of the reckless behaviour shown by officials and parents. Walter said he has the right to remove officials and put them behind the barrier. "We report it to the Belgian FA and then they will be issued a fine and if it happens again they can get a touchline ban". Also in Belgium, they have a great dropout of referees of which most are the younger breed. "The things they have to hear, the verbal abuse and sometimes the physical abuse is increasing more and more".

## Across the pond...

Fernando, in the land of stars and stripes, reported on the BBC forum that what people fail to see, is that for every million children who play the game at youth level, maybe one will go on to play at a higher level (the chances are slightly higher Fernando but we take your point), and that is in the UK where opportunities abound – the chances are even less in the States where soccer is just taking off. Parents need to understand that not every kid is the next Ronaldo and if they are successful, it can only happen by appreciating the amount of hard work and dedication it takes.

The pressure is that of a sauna every time a player crosses that white line. It's not surprising that so many quit the game. A minority make it through, with many quitting football at a young age. The facts are there, and while you ponder, think of how many young footballers you know who play for fun, and reflect on how many you know that may make it into the professional game, or are already there. The town I live in boasts only one player still playing in the professional game in the Championship. Our town (Bridlington) has produced a wealth of talent over the years, including players that have represented local schools of excellence, academies, non league clubs, professional clubs and coached all over the world. Our town is not different to many others, and the fine line of success and failure is there to see.

Steve in Houston, USA, coached American Youth Soccer for five years. As a British expat he thought that it would not be as competitive, nor have extreme parental involvement as in the U.K. How wrong. Parents are fanatical in the support and wanting results for the team and their own child. Steve had a t-shirt made with the words on the back: "I coach, you cheer, no questions". He has seen parents fighting at games where poor decisions by the referee were considered the reason the game was lost. Needless to say, Steve was the object of parents' frustration and anger, if their child was not selected or played a bad game. In America, the goals are just as rewarding and with scholarships on offer for colleges and universities, lower fees for the parents can hinge on players performances. As daft as it sounds, I'm sure you are thinking by now – "I'm glad it does happen overseas, as if it was just solely us, then the worry would be almost unthinkable."

Also in the States, Thom said he finds this display of violence and misconduct that is happing in England very amusing. Thom remarked that when his kids were learning soccer (football) from English coaches, they would tell him and others of the non involvement of parents in youth soccer in England. The US had many incidents of the type described in this book and he also wrote a program called S.A.G.E. "SET A GOOD EXAMPLE".

**Research studies in America found that 90% of young performers would rather play on a losing team than sit on a bench of a winning team – more proof that it is the participation that counts.**

Violence and abuse in youth sports generally has escalated to an alarming level in the USA and news reports like the examples below are not uncommon. From parents tackling opposing players to threatening coaches with firearms to physical fights resulting in arrests, it's not always fun and games in the world of youth soccer:

"A 42 year-old adult man strikes the soccer referee, who happened to also be the town's mayor, during a match between 11-year-old girls. The coach was sentenced to one year in jail (all but 45 days was suspended), required to attend anger management courses and banned from all youth sports events for a year."

The American Youth Soccer Organization (AYSO) banned one parent and two soccer coaches for life and disbanded two boy's soccer teams following the worst brawl in its 35-year history. About 30 adults were involved in a post-match melee in the southern California town of San Juan Capistrano after a tournament game between the Palmdale Eagles and the Chino Chiefs. Three adults were arrested, one parent needed treatment for a bite, another suffered cuts and a swollen eye and others reported being hit on the head with umbrellas and being threatened by a man swinging a metal rod. The cause of the melee after the San Juan Capistrano game was unclear but reports from the sheriff's department at the time said violence broke out after an assistant coach for the winning team allegedly tried to pick a fight with a losing player.

In 2006 still in the USA, two soccer coaches got into a fistfight at a game for 7-year-old girls; a youth football coach attacked a referee; and another coach went after a 13-year-old opponent. Alarmingly a parent allegedly pulled a .357 Magnum at a football game for 5 and 6-year-olds as he argued over playing time for his son. I'm glad I got out when I did.

"The structure of team sports is outdated and broken," says Scott Lancaster of Somers, N.Y., the senior director of youth football development for the National Football League and author of Fair Play, a book that aims to take the negatives out of youth sports and encourages positive parental involvement. "Preconditioning children to value only final results in sports competitions robs them from the joy of spontaneous play and learning new skills in a positive environment." It's a great read and is written with the same ethos as this book.

Lancaster believes it is the way that youth sports are organised, taught and implemented that is at the very root of the problem: "Kids are forced to play adult versions of games to satisfy an 'adult' thirst for experiencing what they watch on television."

Often the emphasis is on winning at all costs. Parental behaviour at youth sports events often teaches our children that confrontation and cheating is the way to resolve conflict.

The following report on an incident in the US, shows how youth football incidents can escalate. This story made mainstream news:

When teenage boys start fighting and the fists start flying, it is instinctive for parents to run over and try and break up the dispute, especially if their own children are in the middle of the brawl. For the first 45 minutes, it had been an ordinary soccer game when the 14-years-old-and-under Downtown United boys played against the Brooklyn Italians. But in the 46th minute, as DUSC manager Deb Cook looked down for just a second, a fight erupted among the players, resulting in a call to 911 and the subsequent arrest of a parent.

The game had begun with steady rain and disgruntled parents at opposite ends of the field. Both teams had been plagued by rain and cancellations all season, and even though an official referee did not show up, everyone wanted to get this game over with, except for Litzia Iodannis, who knew better, and adamantly advised not to play this game. Iodannis, mother of Fannis, had seen games spin out of control and get ugly without a licensed referee. "It all happened so fast. I looked up and I was shocked," said DUSC's Cook, describing seeing players from both sides attacking each other. At moments like this a qualified referee would have taken control of the game by penalizing and ejecting players by giving yellow and red cards. However, what kid was going to listen to an untrained parent referee who didn't even carry red cards in his back pocket?

"How did this start, anyway?" some of the players were asking when the melee was finally over. It had been a 1-1, when DUSC forward Michael Rafty claimed that a Brooklyn Italian player pulled his shirt one too many times, which became so annoying that he gave his opponent a brisk shove back, which is not uncommon. Sometimes worthy of a yellow card, sometimes not, and is often done when a ref is not looking. By all eyewitness accounts, in a split second a few more kids jumped in swinging, when Brooklyn Italians goalie Angel Cordero came out of the net in defence of his players, only to get a whack in the face and a bloody nose. Parent Vasill Rafty, known as Bill, was already out on the field with the boys, when several other parents from both teams darted onto the pitch to try and stop the fight.

The only thing manager Cook could hear was people yelling at the top of their lungs to get off the field. "In a moment, it had escalated beyond belief!" added Cook.

"When I saw my kid on the floor crying, that's when I knew I had to do something," said Joe Caruana, a Brooklyn Italian parent, explaining why he ran onto the field to help his son Joey who had been grabbed on the back of the neck and thrown to the ground. Within minutes the dust had settled and as the fighting ended, both parents and players were seething and casting blame, all in agreement that the Cosmopolitan League had let them down by not ensuring a certified referee would be there to officiate. Next, Caruana took his son and goalie Cordero to the local security office to call the police. The boys fully understood the gravity of accusing a parent of assault as they recounted the incident with police officers from the Sixth Police Precinct. They identified "the man in the green jacket" as the person who assaulted them which resulted in the arrest of DUSC parent Rafty.

The Sixth Police Precinct confirmed that Rafty was arrested and charged with third-degree assault. According to reports, he was led off the field in handcuffs.

However, Cook insisted that Rafty did not punch anyone. "His own kid was at the bottom of a pile of kids and he went in to pull him out of harm's way," said Cook.

It is no surprise that 22 players and even more parents on a rainy night had significantly different accounts of what actually happened. But they all agreed that this game should never have been played without a licensed referee for the teenage boys. Even responsible adult players push the envelope on the pitch without a referee, with a few extra shirt pulls and shoves, maybe even an illegal trip, knowing they can get away with it. Ironically, veteran referee Manny D'Almeida was upstairs on a nearby smaller rooftop field coaching girls, unaware of the fight down in the courtyard.

"This would never have happened with a good referee," said D'Almeida, shaking his head. "I encourage players to play hard and tough, but punching is an automatic red card, and I immediately eject that player from the game," said D'Almeida, who has overseen many high-testosterone games that could have easily gotten out of hand.

Predictably the rest of the U-14 boys game was cancelled, ending on a sour note, as players and parents refused to finish the match. In retrospect, parents from both sides conceded that although it is counterintuitive to stand still and stay on the sidelines when a fight breaks out, it is thoroughly counterproductive to run onto the field and get involved.

"Where my daughter plays in New Jersey, there is a policy of zero tolerance for disruptive behaviour and that goes for both players and parents," remarked Joe Caruana, noting this would have never happened in his daughter's league. He agreed that in this day and age parents all too often fuel disruptive behaviour among the players with hot-headed mindless yelling from the sidelines.

Raymond is an Englishman and is quite appalled about the behaviour of parents he has read about within grassroots football. It reminded him of when living in Canada watching parents fighting at Hockey games involving 12 year old players...unbelievable! Regarding football, Ray has been refereeing football in the USA (North Carolina, South Carolina & Florida) for 5 years at adult, high school & youth club levels. He reported he has rarely seen anything that resembles the behaviour shown in the UK and the reports.

Ray describes the club he officiates at in Northern Florida (Creeks Soccer Club). "The club has 1800 kids and 10 soccer fields, each field is furnished with small aluminium seating stands for the parents with 3 or 4 levels of seating that is located 2 meters from the touchline. The stands are always located opposite the team benches, parents are only allowed in this area." Regarding verbal abuse, it is not allowed by the club, the parents sign a charter that they will follow all club rules and are encouraged to only offer positive support to their children and their team and criticism of the opposition or officials is not tolerated. Other features of the club are that alcohol is not allowed and they provide food and refreshments (a good source of revenue for the club). The club also has a large play area and picnic facilities to support a pleasant family atmosphere along with a paid field marshal who is responsible to ensure all club rules are being enforced. However, high school games are quite different, with parents constantly hurling abuse at the officials; in this case it is mostly lack of knowledge of the rules ... Ray looks at it as being like a "rock star". You are centre stage... the lights are on you...you blow your whistle and they scream at you!

His points are valuable and clearly share the same message as the Respect campaign. Sign the register, stand in the allocated areas and enjoy. The parents are all part of the day and need to contribute where possible. Not just turn up to be entertained for the hour, thinking the paying of their annual subscriptions is a ticket for every match.

## At the top of Europe

The April 2011 Champions League semi-final between Barcelona and Real Madrid was billed as the El Classico derby of the decade. It let itself down as players, tactics and the coaches clashed, giving UEFA a "respect" headache. These two clubs, leaders in world football, gave us 90 minutes of diving, cheating and clearly showed no respect for each other, the competition and the watching billions. The problems are clearly there worldwide from the top to the bottom, and are interesting how each country deals with the perpetrators. The Spanish module is been driven as one to follow, though this game will have cast doubts over it by some quarters.

# THE DISRESPECT TIMES

**Breaking news down under...**

**TWO fathers and a junior coach faced fight charges stemming from a violent brawl after an under-11's soccer match.**

In April 2011 Safaa Rofa'el, 38, and brother Alaa Rofa'el, 33, allegedly got into an argument with Mounties junior soccer club coach Said Ayari, 48, following the team's 3-1 win at Hoxton Park Reserve in Hinchinbrook, in Sydney's south west.

In front of dozens of parents and children, Ayari then allegedly produced scissors that he had retrieved from his car, and Safaa Rofa'el grabbed a folding chair and used it to hit the coach, before the three men began brawling.

Police arrested the men at the park and they were charged with a variety of offences. The brothers pleaded not guilty in Liverpool Local Court.

*Crazy ...*

And finally, here are some views from the rest of the United Kingdom. Not strictly abroad but a different FA governing body nonetheless.

Excerpts taken from the Scottish Sunday Mail…

**Pushy parents need to stop instilling fear into young footballers, says SFA chief Gordon Smith**

Gordon Smith is backing a nationwide drive to stamp out the pushy parents and football coaches who are crushing kids' confidence by screaming from the sidelines.

The SFA chief executive is all too familiar with the scene played out every Saturday on public pitches - having witnessed helpers doing more harm than good as a young player AND a father.

And from the moment Smith was approached by fellow dads to ask why he was not shouting at son Grant – who went on to play for Carlisle - he knew the culture had to change.

If we are ever going to shrug off our reputation for physical, kick-and-rush football Smith insists we must start by removing the deep-rooted fear factor he believes is drummed into our kids.

The heroes of tomorrow aren't going to produce creative football if they are too scared to put their foot on the ball because grown men are shouting at them to hoof it.

He said: "Football can be quite hard on kids and that comes from coaches and parents shouting at them a lot and being critical.

"It's part of the Scottish culture that people are exceptionally critical, especially in football, and I've experienced that.

"I remember going to watch Grant when he was 10 or 11 and some of the parents asked: 'Why don't you shout at your boy? We all do it so why don't you?'".

I told them I would talk to him when he got home but meantime I would let him enjoy playing the game. A lot of parents think they are doing their best for the kid and don't realise the damage they are doing.

Maybe that's a deep-rooted contributor to the frantic nature of Scottish football.

Maybe it's why our game is based on tackling instead of concentrating more on the technical side."

"In Finland they have a saying 'Don't shout at the boy on the ball - he's busy'."

"The message we're trying to get across is parents and coaches should develop kids as people and not just players."

For more info visit www.positivecoachingscotland.com

The following extracts are some interesting experiences of youth football in Scotland that users of a football forum have shared.

"I remember playing in boys football some time ago now, against a top of the league side. We got stuffed, as expected, but every time a goal was scored, whether it was my fault or not, one of the parents had it in for me and kept shouting and saying how useless I was. I remember this game mostly because of all the abuse from her was directed at me. On numerous other occasions the referee had sent her from the sidelines, which in Scotland, although it maybe doesn't happen enough, does happen. Referees should have the authority to send off idiot parents giving no encouragement, only abuse. The boy whose parent it was became very embarrassed due to his mothers antics. So not only did I feel bad but her son felt terrible as well. If parents feel the need to voice their opinion it should be done in a constructive manner, encouraging the young lads to do better."

"My son plays at under 13 level in Scotland and has played since he was 5 years old......the state of youth football north of the border is not much better than England. It's not just the parents who give abuse from the sidelines, some of the coaches involved in the game are not fit to run a subbuteo team never mind coach young children. I know of some teams who have three and four coaches who constantly shout abuse at opposing teams and officials, in one game a coach threatened the parents of the opposing team."

Across the water in Ireland:

"I am a coach in Ireland. We have something called Kickstart, which is run by the FAI with professional coaches. It is aimed at coaching the coaches and bringing the fun element back in to youth football. It covers everything from child welfare to how to deal with parents and has coaching cards etc. to help with the coaching. We have non competitive leagues (try telling the kids it's non competitive!) and the results are not posted in the media. In our club we have meetings with the parents before the season kicks off, where they are told exactly what is expected of them, if there are any issues during games the coach would speak to that parent and if necessary, that child would not be selected again. We don't seem to have any problems in our league."

I have coached myself in Northern Ireland, in Belfast. I felt at ease with the whole set up, and found the level of expectancy more acceptable than what I had been used to. Through Bobby Charlton's soccer schools I coordinated a summer camp at Campbell College in the heart of the city. The place had a different vibe to it, and although I never had the chance to see the players play in teams during the season, the atmosphere was almost surreal in contrast to the intensity at home. The Milk Cup is held there each year which is for youth team players from clubs all over the world, from

Manchester United to Queens Park in Scotland, to Mexican and Brazilian academies. There seems to be a feel in Ireland that is different to any I've been involved in, and that football at a young age is meant to be a pleasurable experience, to have fun and enjoy.

## And finally in Wales...

The chairman of the Aberystwyth and District Junior League, where 56 teams play each week during the season, involving approximately 700 local children, reported he had been following the debate on Sky Sports News. Fortunately he commented they have very few problems either from coaches or parents. All coaches must have a Football Leaders Coaching Award and all team must be accredited. The latter requires clubs to have player, parent and coaching codes of conduct. All under 11 games are non competitive in the sense that results are not collated and there are no league tables. The U13 and U15 leagues are competitive. The non-competitive games are no less exciting and it does not have any effect on the game other the children enjoying the game. He commented "Perhaps we are fortunate but things seem to work here, but a lot is down to clear guidelines on appropriate behaviour, appropriate training, codes of conduct, and people accepting standards. We are clear that we will not tolerate poor behaviour or over zealous managers."

Also in Wales during my research I found that many leagues and clubs had created better atmospheres and incorporated a lot of the new ideas the English FA have wanted to introduce. I'm sure there have been problems in Ireland and Wales, though they will be happy to hear that I couldn't find any...

I've coached in Newport again for Bobby Charlton's, and all I remember is the eagerness of the kids to learn and develop new skills. They played with a smile and eagerness to learn from the coaching staff.

Stop Press! Maybe the Welsh aren't perfect after all. A report from North Wales in 2010 tells us…

"A player in a North Wales cup tie was given 4 red cards. Stamped on an opposition player.  Argued with the ref. Soaked the ref with water. Threatened the ref in the clubhouse.
The North Wales Coast Football Association suspended the player for two years and fined him £75."

There's always one isn't there?

The Burlington Jackdaws and coaches for 2009

La Forza girls in 1999

Lily Mae with Ian Dowie and Jay Cochrane and Tim Lees

The Jackdaw Under 11s celebrate winning the Simon Tindall memorial trophy

Lily Mae in action

Sister Bronte in action for the same team

Louis Beckett with coach Adam Ykhlef , after collecting the club player of
the season award after signing for Hull City.

The author in 2011 after the clubs presentation in which he received Man
United's new home shirt for his work in season 2010-11

The author with Jackdaws keeper of the Year… Joshua Brown

The Burlington Jackdaws Under 9s 2009 featuring Lily Mae and Callum
Cobden

# PART THREE

### Get Back - The Beatles 1968

## My Story...

Returning to England in 2001 was something that I always intended to do, with a back pack of experience and knowledge. I embarked on a journey around the country, to watch junior games and compare my own coaching standards to what I was witnessing. I was stunned at the lack of order on our pitches and sidelines, and found it hard to identify exactly who were the coaches, as an army of mums and dads patrolled the touchlines issuing instructions to their boy/girl and the rest of the team.

My original plan was to look at coaching jobs, though didn't think I would get involved with this state of affairs and end up running a junior football team. (How wrong I would be?).

I developed soccer training schools, camps and training sessions locally and a journey began to unfold. By using the reputation of being in the USA, I built up a large database of players from the ages of 4-16 who simply wanted to play football for fun. Manchester United Soccer Schools along with Bobby Charlton Soccer Schools were both very helpful in my career, as I obtained work through both companies. Touring the country and coaching youngsters in the UK, including residential camps, allowed me to meet great coaches, players and people. I also coached at a School of Excellence, at a club now not in league action and could see a pleasurable difference between all of this compared to the recklessness of junior football. The junior clubs in the North East and West seemed to have teams that were either geared up to win, or simply hanging by a thread with a depleted team – one extreme or the other. The problem was there to see, and through the coaching programmes I coordinated, I proceeded to enter the fray and develop a local junior club with a real difference.

I researched what was going on not only in this country but also around Europe, where coaching methods and grassroots football seemed to be operating differently. In Holland, 'Total' football was also met with 'Total' tolerance on the touchlines. In some cases the parents were totally exempt from watching their child's development, with clubs preferring to feedback later instead. It seemed in England that winning and not enjoyment was the target for those involved in the junior game and it was almost unheard of for a junior team to be able to just play and relax. The pressure cooker atmosphere at this level in England was not helped by big clubs beginning to circle around players as young as 8 – with potential riches on the horizon.

In 2010 Chelsea demonstrated their faith in the old adage "if you're good enough, you're old enough" by signing an 11-year-old boy from the club who occupied the 90th rung on the professional game's 92-club ladder. For Michael Gyasi, a promising German-born striker who had spent a little over two years at Northampton Town's centre of excellence, this was the stuff of dreams.

Gyasi first crossed Chelsea's radar in 2009, when he travelled south to play for Northampton Under-10s against their counterparts from the Chelsea academy. After a further appearance against them, Chelsea's recruitment staff asked whether Gyasi could come to train with them. He did so during the summer holidays and impressed to such a degree that the club set in motion moves to sign him.

Chelsea paid compensation to Northampton for their development of the schoolboy, and it is believed that a down-payment of not more than £10,000 had been negotiated. The football authorities prefer clubs to resolve such issues between themselves rather than resort to arbitration. Further payments would be due to Northampton if Gyasi becomes a scholar or turns professional.

Northampton appeared delighted at the money coming to them, which they said would aid their youth development programme but in broader terms, the deal seemed to illustrate just how competitive the market for players has become, even for ones who are so young.

"I think this is a trend that is going to happen," Trevor Gould, the head of Northampton's centre of excellence said.

It was certainly a trend that I saw emerging as academies set up shadow squads in other areas, as they began to 'tap up' players even as young as 4. Mini soccer had created a monster, as more and more kids began to have aspirations to play for Arsenal, Chelsea, or Liverpool, at such a young age. Why wouldn't they, or shouldn't they play for them? They may only be 7 years old but other children their age were already earning contracts.

Back to my coaching research, I was informed that at West Bromwich Albion, they had come up with what they called a 'Pig Pen' where the spectators were asked to view some 200 yards from the game. At Charlton, there was to be no second chances and anyone who didn't toe the line would be kicked out, along with their player, however talented. They just would not accept it.

Junior and mini soccer leagues seemed to be as competitive as any amateur league. I observed many games, one day being told a match was top versus bottom and similar unnecessary hype. Probably the greatest line that day was when I heard this quote:

**"You've come to watch a real treat here. We hate them, they hate us, it'll be mental mate!"**

This was a "local derby" between two teams from the same club at the same age group!

I thought long and hard and ensured the right people were involved from the off. A club with fully qualified coaches, with barriers up along the side, and with parent's helping voluntarily like in the States with the administration work. A club that made a difference and players developing more holistically rather than to win at all costs. Some parents involved seemed bemused by it, other clubs and the league surprised by the way it was being directed. I'd swallowed a few coaching manuals, bitten a load of ideas from professional clubs and digested a blueprint for junior football for the future. I knew that things could and would only change for the better. Our youngest team didn't even enter a league and simply played games, though because of the apparent lack of contest, we did lose players, though that was always going to happen.

We also introduced a club phone, so the coaches were not pestered by parents, and one central phone line gave the club the chance to digest the information before replying or dealing with any incident.

The club would also work, train and play together and have club fun tournament days. They wouldn't separate off into different pockets and have their own funds, presentation evenings and have different rules.

The club would quite simply sing from the same hymn sheet.

I'm not claiming we were the first, as I know there were many other clubs already set up with a similar ethos of helping to educate the future of English football. Junior football is of course the most important part of the football community, and with the combined efforts of clubs and local support we can be confident that our children are given the best chance to become better players.

I once read of a club who entered no leagues and played mini tournaments with their squads of players every weekend, mixing up the teams, and all flowed with no problems.

Many have implemented some of the ideas that help us build a better future for our young talent. The FA's new initiatives with 25 proposals feature in the Future Game paper and ex-Middlesbrough boss Gareth Southgate was put in charge of the new scheme. The proposals are still being received by County FAs and leagues, who are then cascading the information to clubs and the players, with a view to being implemented in September 2011.

In spite of my concerns about parents on the touchlines, I decided to forge ahead with my plans to bring a new club into the area. East Riding League representative and fantastic servant of local club Bridlington Rangers, John Gibson MBE informed me: "Teams are folding all over the place, because of a new culture spreading into junior football. They simply would rather sit at home and play computer games in the comfort of their own home, where they are safe and warm." He welcomed my idea of bringing another club into the town to help give the children more opportunities and I take this chance to thank John for his initial support.

I found children in the UK no longer play enough football; consequently they are not as fit as they used to be. The old traditional breeding methods - the street game, playing football in the playground, tennis balls, kicking the ball against a wall, along with regularly playing alongside and against bigger lads - have been replaced by only playing these games in the comfort of their own homes on Playstations, Wii's, Xboxes and handheld consoles. Therefore we no longer have a proper foundation. Modern technology and a more affluent society have inevitably played a big part in this loss as the Xbox generation are more likely to play a game of "FIFA" then go outside for a game of headers and volleys. These consoles exist in Germany and Spain and they don't seem to have the problems the UK does – is technology too easy an explanation?

Most drop out of the game totally by the age of 21, and leagues and the FA's around the country have noticed the decline and introduced Under 20/21 leagues to maintain participation. Why are young players dropping out? And why do they not want to play the sport that they have enjoyed since maybe the age of 4 or 5? Drop out is all too common and it could be due to failure or complete loss of faith in the game. Up to the age of ten you may have played for the local side, then from 10 until 14 you were playing with an academy team, signing forms and featuring in the local press. At 14 you are released, you are in Year 10 at school, your GCSEs arrive and you haven't a clue having spent the last four years journeying the country in the back seat of your dad's car. You leave school with nothing, back at your local club; your only option at 17 is to play for a mate's dad's team, who hail you as their star player. A fiver a week in subscription fees, grown men kicking lumps out of you, followed by a few beers after the game. You've soon had enough of this, so it's an early retirement with no qualifications by the age of 21.

I'll say it again: don't you think it's alarming, that players fall out of love with the game as they get older? Something has been put in place by the FA and they have a scheme called Get Into Football directed at the 18-21 age group.

There is still no excuse for the current European statistics: the UK has the unfittest kids in Europe; the UK has the least number of PE hours per week in Europe; the UK has the most obese kids per population ratio in Europe; in the UK, kids, on average, spent 85% of their time indoors, the highest level in Europe.

The parents see the high profile of the players in the Premier League and dream that their child will emulate this, though the worrying statistic is that a tiny minority actually make the grade. In reality, the chances of success are very slim indeed.

The concern is where players end up and I've seen some lads I've known well, fall on the scrap heap. Now this may not be parental pressure, just a sense of failure that makes people do crazy things.

I'm proud to have played a small part in the progress so far but I'll be further pleased when I see a lot more young players being able to play in a safe, friendly environment; under no pressure from adults and protected to some degree from the pitfalls that they may encounter. Would you have ever thought that Man United would not sign a player because he couldn't run a bath; or young players would be led to drink and drugs due to pressure...? Stop and pause for a minute before you read on about the pitfalls in the game.

Not making it in football can be a journey in itself and I was concerned that if you didn't reach the grade, then do you have something else up your sleeve? Or were the parents so focussed on chasing the dream that they had ignored any school progress, along with the kids not having a part time job, due to their football commitments at the weekend (a link to the working world they would soon be entering). Even among the elite players I had my concerns: are we turning the children into clones of each other and stifling their creativity on the ball?

In the 70's when football was in its golden era, every child mattered and would play regardless of age and ability. If you wanted to play, you could. There were no barriers of age, ability, gender or anything else. 20 a side games were often seen in parks, with no adult around in a tracksuit or sheepskin coat shouting the odds about positions or tactics. It was real fun they had then, with fewer cars on the road and less stories of people preying on the children.

Nowadays, as we have touched on many times already, some parents expect their player to grace the Wembley turf. I felt if I was to set up this club and make it work then there must be a clear pathway from starter to club football and club to academy level. With it came the birth of a small Charter Standard football club who can now boast 6 teams, with a starter programme with a register of 30 children, along with 4 players going on to play for Hull City along with a player representing the East Riding School representative team. We fall a long way short of other clubs in numbers, though it shows it can be done from scratch, with the correct methods used and demonstrated. My plan was to let our children learn by their mistakes and express themselves and allow them to get it right or wrong, and above all make football fun.

### Keep the Faith – Bon Jovi 1999

Football can provide structure, routine and discipline in a young person's life. In some cases, this can be a stark contrast to a chaotic home life that some kids have to endure. Being part of a well organised club is a great way to learn life skills such as discipline, team work and respect. What are the alternatives to a Tuesday night football practice? Some are equally as beneficial (other sports clubs, volunteering) but others can lead to a rapid downward spiral for some individuals (hanging around parks and shops due to "boredom"; a cigarette, a swig of cider, a few "dares" to pass the time).

Football isn't everyone's cup-of-tea but it's a crying shame that some young players leave the game when, in the right environment, they would have happily continued.

The following stories are not about players who left the game due to excessive pressure and I hope that they are both isolated cases and not the norm. However, both demonstrate worst case scenarios of young players lost to the game. The point is – let's not push kids out when the outside world is not always a nice place to be.

There is a harrowing story from concerning a young ex-Newcastle player aged 19, who had progressed through youth football alongside Michael Owen.

Jamie Burt was caught stealing from the players' dressing room and he confessed to a growing drug habit. The then Newcastle United manager (Kevin Keegan) did not want to end the talented youngster's career before it had really begun, so gave Burt another chance. Though it was too late. Jamie was already in the grip of an addiction which led to his conviction for supplying and conspiracy to supply heroin and cannabis. It was a far cry from the days when he set up the winning goal for Michael Owen in a schoolboy International against Brazil before 33,000 fans at Wembley. But while Owen went on to become the golden boy of English football, Jamie sank into a life of petty crime.

Yes, we are getting off the beaten track a little, though the dangers are there and this story demonstrates that. Jamie did get back to playing football and went onto play for Chesterfield, Scarborough and Whitby Town

There is another story similar to this of a player called John Courtney, also on the books of Newcastle as a youngster.

(excerpt taken from the Independent)

"John Courtney was only three when Eileen Clarke, a nursery teacher, first set eyes on him kicking a ball on his own in the corner of a playground in Newcastle upon Tyne's East End. She instinctively knew he was special.

"I've seen a smashing little player," she told her husband, Brian, one of the city's best known football scouts. Mr Clarke, who has discovered prodigies including Paul Gascoigne, Lee Clark, Robbie Elliott and Shola Ameobi, turned his nose up at first but his wife's instincts 18 years ago turned out to be right.

John graduated to Newcastle United's school of excellence where Mr Clarke, whose reputation is dependent on not exaggerating talent, considered him "another Alan Shearer".

But it was not to be. John Courtney's parents buried him at the age of 21. They released images of him as he was found dead: slumped half-dressed on a carpet, clutching a final heroin fix."

These stories could happen to anyone, and it makes me sick when you see the media making a celebrity out of known addicts such as Pete Doherty. With Pete regularly pictured with Kate Moss on his arm (when they were couple) this can only serve to glamourise heroin to youngsters.

John was to be the next Alan Shearer and Jamie had seen Michael Owen go on to play for Liverpool, Newcastle, Real Madrid and Manchester United. It's such a fine line, and when you hear of boys being released at 9 and 10 from academies you hope they don't fall out with the game. It's a frightening proposition for a young footballer, and if we want to retain football as our national sport and be proud of its achievement within the world, then it will take a lot more than the FA to resolve all the issues - the Government, Local Authorities, schools, and parents all need to get their act together.

These pitfall stories are very harrowing. Youngsters that don't make it are often shipped around the country in backs of cars from one club to another. Every Boys Dream written by Chris Green (who I met at the Grassroots show in Birmingham) shows and demonstrates the concerns he has for the generation of youngsters who are released from clubs. His book, which I purchased and often speak about, gives an insight into the harrowing stories and he doesn't pull any punches. Boys who give up everything and end up with nothing. Parents who spend thousands on fuel collecting more Esso vouchers than their wallet can hold; new cars to make the journey more comfortable; leaving work early and losing out on over-time and loss of pay; eating tea out of service stations, McDonalds or heated up at bedtime in the microwave. The costs, both financial and quality of life, are huge.

I was once told of player who was at Leeds United from the age of 8, all the way to 16. He was never advised, nor were his parents, of what would happen if he never made it into the white shirt at Elland Road. During those eight years he had missed out on playing with his pals and his school life was affected so much so that he left with nothing despite being a bright kid.

Whilst coaching for Manchester United Soccer Schools, I was asked to stay in the accommodation where our French players were staying. We were asked to keep a keen eye on one lad in particular, as United had been given a tip off about this lanky French boy. He was in my group and he excelled. He simply looked the business. Though 3 days in, I noticed he was wearing the same gear, and began to smell a little, as did a few others. On returning to our lodgings I investigated the shared bathroom, and noticed that only I had used the small bath (as there was no shower) which left me concerned. Speaking very little French I proceeded to ask the boys if they had used the bathroom, to which they laughed out loud...

It turned out they simply didn't know how to run a bath, and without a shower, they went without washing. The session that evening was cancelled as I went through a demonstration of running such a luxury. Needless to say, Day 4 , 5 and 6 , I couldn't get in the place as the French sat for hours singing and relaxing in this new found home comfort.

Now United had been looking at this lad, who could play football, but seemed unable to look after himself.

It could have cost him, who knows... I don't know whether he did go on and make the grade but his name was Thierry so he had great namesake to follow. United had apparently lost interest with the feedback they received of his inability to look after himself. They scrutinise a players every move and in the weeks leading up to signing Andy Cole, they had also been heavily linked with Chris Sutton, who was firing in goals with Norwich City. Cole was favoured ahead of Sutton who was watched intensely for two weeks, his every move was watched by a United representative.

Boys leave home to become stars without basic hygiene qualities and can fail. They don't know how to cook, clean or look after money, all traits needed if one becomes successful.

Stories emerge of players who were homesick, and I heard of a player who returned home for the love of his girlfriend, even though Kevin Keegan (ex England manager, Liverpool legend) had told him he had a future at the club. Lee Carsley's form dipped so much so at Birmingham City, that the club looked into why this could have happened. On further inspection, they found he had moved to the area and lived alone. He couldn't cook and lived out of silver foil trays from the Chinese. The club ensured a cook was assigned to Carsley and his form was resurgent.

Fabian Delph moved from Leeds United to Aston Villa for a large fee at 19 and was put into what locals regarded as a "haunted" hotel. His form dipped completely. He became homesick (understandably so) and was moved nearer home. In the 80's I remember Man United players Ryan Giggs and Lee Sharpe being hosted by local families, who would take the boys in and pamper them as though they were at home with mum. You can see the benefits of this in their respective footballing careers and some might suggest Sharpe went off the boil when his teenage curfew ended! I once met Lee after bumping into him on a night out in Newcastle. Decent bloke! Great autobiography!

Cristiano Ronaldo signed for United at 19 and his mum moved over with him to help with his cooking, cleaning and general well being. On the flip side, Marco Ballotelli moved to neighbours City and was put into a high rise apartment in the middle of Manchester, seemingly alone. Ballotelli has never been far from controversy including setting off fireworks from his high rise lodgings and apparently being a regular at the local restaurants.

It must be a worry for all parents, when a big club comes knocking and their offspring have to move away from home at the age of 14 in some cases (outside the UK thankfully). Will they survive? In Barcelona they have produced footballer after footballer and their current crop all came though their centre of excellence, looked after and simply mollycoddled at their fantastic facilities.

**One Dad told me that when taking his son to find out whether or not he was being kept on for another season, he turned to his son to ask him if he knew where he was going? "To find out if I'm getting sacked Dad!" the 10 year old replied.**

Fortunately he wasn't sacked and carries on with the club and at ten years old, I hope he never has that feeling. I guess they hear of managers being sacked all the time and see that as a guide. Not good enough and your out. Those immortal words of "Sorry son, you're not good enough, come back another day" must not only be heart breaking for the kid but the parent too. How do they face their school pals? How do they go back into their junior team and nick poor old little Johnny's place at left back, who has been standing in since the day he left?

We are talking about a very few children chasing limited options. Some kids think they are already footballers before they have begun and believe they are going to be rich. Being released at 8 is a lot easier than at 15, with more time to recover. Jim White described the system as brutal and said in a piece in the Telegraph:

**"The shedding of people at 16 has always been footballs hidden secret. Axing kids hasn't improved been improved by the academy system, and if anything has got worse"**

There is also the shadow squad concept that has emerged. To those not familiar with them, shadow squads are set up in order to recruit more players in different areas. Tottenham has 10 shadow squad centres, basically waiting rooms, for those potentially earmarked as talented but are too young or not ready to be signed up for the academy. There were 600 boys in the 10 centres in 2009. In 2010, 20 players were signed-on from this system, leaving 580 players disappointed, along with mums and dads. The club's will argue that the 580 have had a better standard of coaching. I've seen a similar set up and the kids actually played in the kits and under the clubs banner. My concern with the whole procedure is that most of these centres are in a place that will require a car to get to. Does this mean the parents who can't drive get overlooked as the Dad with the flashy wheels ensures his kid is first in the queue for any such trial.

Academies and sessions set up using the clubs badge are always under attack.

"Opportunities [at the top level] are very tight," agrees John McDermott, the then academy head coach at Tottenham who spoke to Sally Williams, in an excellent article on the website ffwtbol.co.uk "Boys have to realise the path is not what it was 10 years ago. You once had to be among the best players in Britain, now you have to be among the best in the world to make it here. Three of the 23 scholars at Tottenham are European (a Swede, an Italian and a Belgian)."

At age 16, the 90-minute travel rule goes out of the window and clubs start to bring in boys and their families from all over the world. "It must be hugely frustrating for kids at English clubs to be told they're not good enough at 16 because of the number of overseas youngsters filling academies," commented Trevor Brooking, the Football Association's director of football development. "When we set up the academy system, I don't think anyone envisaged it would be filled with anything other than Brits."

Sally's work was very inspiring and thought provoking. You may feel that the policies of professional football clubs only apply to a minority of those who play but it affects the majority who think that their kid will make it – the opportunities are decreasing.

In 2007 Watford took the advice from our European counterparts and designed a programme where the club went to school rather than the kids being taken out of the school.

November 2007, and Watford academy under-14s are working out, sprinting the length of the pitch, tracking back and marking. It is 11am on a Thursday morning and the boys should be at school. But they are at school. In September 2007, Watford moved its 11-16-year-olds to Harefield Academy, a secondary school in Uxbridge, west London, arguing that for the club to come to the boys made more sense than the other way around. The boys are picked up from their homes in the morning by special academy buses, coaches come to the school for sessions, special homework clubs are laid on after school, and then the boys are ferried home again for 7.30. This way the boys get to play more football, they say. They also get an education, which is important, said one coach, because "they're more comfortable speaking in front of cameras" (perhaps preparing the kids for a career in acting, should the footie not work out!).

"The academy product is flawed," says Mark Warburton, assistant academy manager and the architect of the new model, based on one at Ajax in Holland. "It involves hours and hours of driving, hours of standing outside watching the boys with the rain lashing down, getting home at half nine or 10, eating meals in the car, being behind on homework, and always being generally tired, because that is what it takes to be a pro footballer – it's always been that way. But it's not that way in Holland, or France. So if it works there and we're buying their players, doesn't that tell you that we've got to change the way we do things?"

It has certainly changed the life of Oli Sprague, 15, and his family. Oli, who lives in Ruislip, was scouted for Queens Park Rangers at age eight, then Chelsea, and now Watford. This means that Oli and his dad, Clinton, 44, a director of an accident management company, have a thorough knowledge of the M40 and M25. This was a problem for his wife and his two other children aged 10 and 6. "Really that amount of travelling started to kill our lives," Clinton says. "It put a lot of strain on the family." But now Watford takes care of it all. "I've got a home life again!" Plus, Oli is less tired, he says, "and incredibly happy playing football."

Every academy is run differently and will have alternative ways of running operations. One man's opinion, is simply not another's, and there are no rights and wrongs in football when talent spotting.

Of course there are many who make it and have great success. In June 2011 Sunderland's Jordan Henderson made a £20 million pound move to Liverpool. He had told his father when he was 8 years old "Dad, I'm gonna be a pro footballer". His Dad, Brian, told The Sun that Jordan does not drink, does not like clubbing and always finds time to go back to his old school for community work. Jordan gave up everything and only has one interest in life, which is football. Brian described how he had brilliant determination and focus. He always reminded him to believe in himself and his talent was never in doubt. Since 2009 Jordan has been part of the England set-up at four levels: Under 19, Under 20, Under 21 and full international.

I've been lucky enough to have coached and worked along some top coaches who all have a story to tell. I'm sure a players success is equally a goal for them, as I know I would love to one day see a player that has come through our system live on Sky Sports. What a buzz that would be, for the parent, player and coach.

For me to see Callum Cobden or Louis Beckett on T.V. would be unreal. Who are these boys, you ask? Hopefully with their development at Hull City, they are players you will know about in the future.

I would also hope that through the tool of football, players who don't make the grade will find other directions in life and fulfill their dreams, rather than be chasing a dream to end up on what can only be described (as I have already) as the scrapheap.

"Talented young footballers do not get the necessary opportunities to prove themselves because of a focus on athleticism and physicality that stems from the adults involved – coaches and parents – taking it all too seriously. The idea that kids' teams must win at all costs as young as the age of 10 or 11 is an overlooked but fundamental spanner in the development works of elite talent in English football, and it's heartening that Southgate recognises the problem."

*Henry Winter - Daily Telegraph*

## The Questions and Answers

## We all have a view!

From those at the top of the game to those at the grassroots level, I put the questions to the coaches I knew and had worked with. The pleasing thing for me was that all of the responses showed a desire for football to move forward collectively.

However, issues do vary from club to club. Brian McClair at Manchester United proclaims teams arrive to play them with one mission - to win! They see the badge and their ears prick up; parents, coaches and players alike. Their attitude changes and the whole approach is different from arrival to kick off. I'm sure United aren't the only club where this happens. From teams at the top of the league, to the local club everyone loves to hate, up and down the country. Sir Alex Ferguson has installed winners into his club. From the 1st team to the youth teams, his theory is everyone wants to beat Manchester United. The winning mentality is also an Italian trait.

On April fool's Day in 2011, The Daily Mail, began a name and shame campaign. The Sportsmail Campaign was called The Stamp It Out campaign and is aimed at clamping down on the abuse of referees by top stars, which has been an ongoing issue.

To introduce the campaign, top-flight bosses were asked for their opinions. Meanwhile, the Premier League plan to draw up new punishments to punish players who transgress, due to be implemented for the 2011/12 season.

Though this book focuses on respect on the touchlines at junior football matches, the research often points the finger at the superstars as the source of disrespect. Therefore, I feel it is worthwhile to consider the thoughts of those at the top, shared in the Daily Mail.

Carlos Anchelotti, when at Chelsea, starts us off and the Italian did not take things lightly. He explains:

"I try to ref every day here in training and there are a lot of people shouting against me. The worst is Nicolas Anelka, who always shouts against me! But I have a big advantage; I don't have a yellow card, I just fine the players. Who gets the money? The manager, of course! Who else would? They shout against me. I've earned a lot of money! Sometimes I try to maintain good control (on the touchline) and it's not easy necessarily to do that.

But if you think it is a problem just in the Premier League, you should look at other games and other leagues. It's worse in Italy, 100 per cent. I don't tell my players that they have to respect the referees because they know that. They know they have to respect the officials and their opponents. That's maybe the first rule of football."

Well Carlo, it's good to hear that it is worse is your native land. He also points to the fact that respect is the first thing players should learn and incorporate. It's a great belief and after watching Chelsea, there appears to be a better respect ethos about their play compared to when Didier Drogba dragged the club through the mire with his conduct in the Champions league on more than one occasion.

In the other corner of London we have Harry Rednapp who has been no stranger to the media. As manager of Tottenham Hotspur he said "It's probably better than it was (players trying to intimidate the referee). If you look back at the 1970s it was the done thing to get round the ref as a group. The most successful teams were known for doing that - the great championship-winning sides - and people said it showed how much they wanted to win"

He was right and Leeds United were portrayed as the main protagonists of this method. The Damned United novel illustrates the issue as Brain Clough takes over the club and explains to the Championship winning squad that they won the trophy by cheating. My own team, Manchester United, were also accused of it in the 90's as Roy Keane and company surrounded referees all over the country trying to influence a decision.

Rednapp continued to explain that players wanted to question decisions all the time but they should be kept away. "You get nothing out of chasing referees. It's very rare that they change decisions so abusing and harassing referees is not a lot of use to anybody and it shouldn't happen. It's not an easy job, so you have to give them all the respect in the world. They do an honest job and sometimes they make mistakes."

"Everyone makes mistakes" Harry added. "What's changed in today's game is that you get a microphone shoved in front of you within 10 minutes of a game finishing. Sometimes you say things on the spur of the moment. I think there should be a cooling-down period and maybe a chance to speak to the referee after the game."

Alex McLeish, when at Birmingham City, impressed upon every player that they needed to adhere to the principles of the Respect campaign. Alex, the former Glasgow Rangers manager, can see that the way players like Roger Johnson now behave towards official's shows they are learning.

"Of course, there is no doubt", Alex concludes, "that we are all aggrieved at refereeing decisions from time to time".

Throughout his own playing career McLeish had a good rapport with referees and tries his utmost not to berate modern-day referees. In his defence, after one of the derbies against Aston Villa, referee Howard Webb told him that the disciplinary side of his Birmingham team was exemplary, which pleased Alex and showed progress is being made.

"You can't hide emotion in football, but it is a difficult job that they [referees] do and we should all try to understand that."

Up in Geordie land, the black white stripes of the toon had seen another managerial change during the 2010-11 season. Alan Pardew thought that the FA's Respect campaign was a noble effort to address some of the issues and some of the pressures the referees are under.

It has highlighted the lack of respect towards officials and more importantly, not just at the professional level, but grassroots too.

Pardew said "The things that go on there are disgusting at times. I go and watch my cousins play and the behaviour of parents, in particular, is awful and that gets down to their sons and daughters. If the campaign has done anything, I hope it has addressed that. I am certainly a bit calmer now. I used to bang on the door a bit more and wanted to strangle a couple of them more regularly. But I am a bit calmer, although not that calm!"

Though Alan is speaking from the business end with his final comments and it is understandable if people aren't pulling their weight. After all, my dad always says, "you go to work, to work" with the difference being it is the managers livelihood, as Paul Ince mentioned earlier when he rebuked the Respect campaign. Ince lost his job not long after his spat.

Arsene Wenger at Arsenal wants more respect.

"Who would disagree with me on that? Never has anybody say they didn't want to be respected. It's a good campaign. You want respect on all fronts and sport has to be an example. We can be inspired by what happens in rugby, for example, but sometimes the referees get too close to the players as well, and they have to keep the right distance with the players."

Arsene is often criticised for blaming and looking for excuses, using officials as his key to failure. Though in his defence, as Harry mentions, Wenger may just say things too quickly and hastily after the game, when emotions are running high. He certainly backs the campaign and it's good to know he is board.

Manchester City's manager Roberto Mancini believes the behaviour of managers and players in the Premier League is very good "If one manager can say his opinion, that is normal."

He thinks that both managers and players behave well and describes that when you play, it is normal that when you are under pressure during the game, a player can say something to the referee.

But, for Mancini, the Premier League is the best league in Europe for behaviour because the players have a lot of respect for the referee, and the same for the managers. Now that is excellent to hear from another Italian manager.

Steve Bruce was part of the United team that were accused of surrounding refs in the 90s and he now feels that there has to be more respect both ways. The former United skipper says officiating is a difficult job and he knows that just from trying to referee on the training ground. "It is always competitive, there are always disputes and it is really hard work. And that's just in training." Says Bruce.

He feels that the Respect campaign worked initially but for some reason we have lost our way and need to find common ground.

Everton have always had an excellent philosophy and I would encourage any coaches to look at their website for coaching pointers. Their manager David Moyes has seen his team get themselves in a lot of situations where they have asked for respect from the referees and he says "asked them to tell us why they have made a certain decision." Moyes feels it needs to be a two way street and Everton have not always been given respect back.

Moyes added "I do actually think managers give referees a lot of respect but I don't think managers get the same back. I'm supposed to sign something every year that is about Respect but I don't know why I sign it. Respect is a word, but people have to earn respect."

Much like the code of conduct and Respect registers at junior football clubs, Moyes has a point. A minority of parents will sign these registers and take away the documents without due consideration. Do they really know what they are, and how it works?

Blackpool were promoted to the Premier League in 2010 much to everyone's surprise, no-one more than myself, who had advised my mate to simply "lump on" them to be relegated that season! Although they were eventually relegated, I took no pleasure in being right after Blackpool had taken the Premier League by storm with their adventurous play. Their charismatic manager Ian Holloway looked at the role of TV in the Respect campaign: "We see referees on a Saturday night and they are wrong. We see camera angles that the fourth official could easily see, could quickly see. Until they actually get that right, I think the game is in a mess. The technology is there but we are not using it. Why not? Let us trial it, let's start it now. Let's get it right. It is complete nonsensical rubbish [that] we can't change it right now. Let's see a smile on everyone's faces, particularly the referees. I would hate to do their job. "

Technology certainly would work if you take two incidents involving goals (and the goal line). Pedro Mendes lobs Roy Carroll at Old Trafford, and the ball quite clearly goes in.
The result - NO GOAL!
Then a tame shot from Frank Lampard (who had previously been denied a sure goal against Germany in the World Cup) beat Spurs keeper Gomez, though he managed to drag the football back, so it didn't cross the line.
The result – GOAL !

One thing's for sure we can't have technology down our local pitch, and as I've already mentioned, it would maybe show the watching crowd how difficult it really is.

After being sacked from Liverpool early in 2011, Roy Hodgson was quickly back in the game with West Bromwich Albion.

Speaking with his usual 'Wasperry Wipple' twang he said:

"No-one in their right mind can argue against it. Of course, we should have a Respect campaign. But maybe one day there will be a campaign also for the public to show some respect. The last person who really went out on a limb to demand respect from the public was Brian Clough. I don't think that football matches are nicer places these days to take your family. I don't believe fans think they have to show respect to anybody, be they players, coaches, the referees - but we never mention that. Maybe one day there will be a campaign for them to show more respect, too."

The views of the managers in the greatest league in the world. Roy Hodgson turns the question round to ask about respect from the fans and the public. It's not just the players and managers who need to show respect - we all need to be singing from the same hymn sheet. As ever, an intelligent view from a man once touted as a potential England manger who has coached extensively at both international and club level in Europe.

Finally the Professional Footballers Association chairman and Burnley player Clarke Carlisle praises the campaign and makes a clear statement

"The truth of the matter is that the actual number of incidents that occur throughout the course of a season is very low. It is just that when those incidents happen the media highlight that and it is blown out of all proportion. Respect has not failed at all."

## New Premier League regulations

To emphasise the importance of the issues driving the Respect campaign, Premier League chief executive Richard Scudamore announced a crackdown on the "unacceptable" behaviour by players and managers towards referees. "The clubs unanimously backed the idea that at the start of season 2011-12 we want to raise the bar," said Scudamore.

The new campaign will target abuse of match officials as well as surrounding the officials; unacceptable criticism of officials; and trying to get opponents sanctioned (i.e. booked or sent off).

The Football Association plus referees and players' groups will be consulted. The 20 top-flight club chairmen have acted after a number of high-profile incidents this season, most recently when Manchester United manager Sir Alex Ferguson received a five-match touchline ban for his television outburst about referee Martin Atkinson after his side's 2-1 defeat at Chelsea on 1 March 2011. Scudamore added:

"I think we do need to concentrate on the player and manager relationship with the referee this time, as every one of us knows that there have been elements of unacceptable behaviour. As to what we think is unacceptable; it's vitriolic abuse towards match officials and that has on occasions gone unpunished; the surrounding of referees is unacceptable; the goading of referees into trying to get opponents sanctioned we think is unacceptable; and also the undue criticism, where it spills over into questioning the referee's integrity or his honesty is also unacceptable." Scudamore said the League Managers' Association has already signalled its support for the campaign. "We are at a point in the game where we do have to rein back from some of this undue criticism of match officials.

The debate will come and we will have it in consultation with managers, and remember the managers are also employed by the clubs so the unanimous support of the clubs today is important."

Scudamore went on to discuss the responsibilities that top players have as role models, an issue I have also highlighted as a massive influence on our young players:

"Footballers enjoy a privileged life. The contrast between what is happening in their world and what is happening in the rest of Britain, and indeed most of the world, is getting starker. Whether it is realistic or not they can't entirely be perfect role models, they are young males and boys can behave badly from time to time. But there is a point where extra responsibility comes with the territory. There are so many good things about what footballers do, so this is not us demonising them. But the mood is that things could improve."

The Premier League will also consult with the Football Association, the Professional Footballers' Association, and then the PGMO body that represents match officials.

Sir Alex was then hit with another charge in May 2011 for the total opposite - praising a referee, Howard Webb, before another game against Chelsea. He was warned again about his future conduct. The rationale for the warning was that he should not talk about referees, whether it be positive or negative.

It baffled the world of football.

## My own survey…

The views of the Premier League managers and those in charge seem to fit nicely with the questions I put to several coaches I had worked with, within different football environments.

The coaches below all work in different capacities, from Steven Taylor and David Bailey at professional clubs to Barry Scott over in the USA (my old boss).

I also received feedback from Elain Fillingham - a girls football coach and PE teacher, and Mike English who runs a company called Sports Club card (I would urge you to look at their website if you are the fundraiser or thinking of raising funds for a local club).

Here are the 6 coaches, as you can see all have different roles, but have the same degree of importance in junior football.

Chris Jenkinson – Level Two Coach, Burlington Jackdaws Under 11 and Scarborough FC Captain.
Steven Taylor - Sheffield Wednesday Football Club.
Barry Scott – USA Michigan Jaguars Technical Director U11-U14.
David Bailey – Bolton Wanderers.
Mike English – Sports Club Card.
Elain Fillingham – Girls PE Teacher Hull.

The questions I put to the 6 coaches were all concerning the Respect campaign and all seemed willing to answer quickly with passion surrounding the subject whilst demonstrating a good understanding of the campaign. I've mixed up the answers for you to mix and match, and to not highlight any problems at any one club.

**What are the worst scenes you have witnessed on a touchline during coaching?**

- During my time coaching – I have witnessed parents being disrespectful to the players of the opposing team, the match officials and also to the parents of opposing team; this sometimes resulting in confrontation on the touchline – this is not the example to be showing the players on the pitch.

- Parents shouting and swearing at the referee and opposition. Players are taken off the field of play if they use bad behaviour. They will possibly not play for the rest of the game. Then either after the match or in training we will discuss the behaviour with the player in the hope of stamping it out. So I agree, the parent should have the same repercussions.

- In Spain I recently saw a coach with an U18s team grab and hit another player on the pitch as he was coaching.

- Parents trying to live their lives through their own children. I witnessed an example of this was recently whilst I was refereeing an under 7s game. One player received so many challenging comments from his own parent, that the pressure led him to start crying. The parent was warned. These seem to be common occurrences which should be dealt with by the club.

- Parents telling their child to 'take out' opponents deliberately.

- Over aggressive, intimidating behaviour from opposition parents and coaches when youngsters make mistakes failing to see that it undermines them.

**2. What are the worst scenes you have witnessed on the field of play?**

- On the field of play – I have witnessed some players and opposing players not performing within the rules of the game, sometimes resulting in foul play. This can then result in fighting on the pitch between players. Being disrespectful to match officials, on some occasions being disrespectful to opposing parents whilst players are on the pitch playing.

- Nothing too serious.

- Punching of an opposing player.

- Fighting between opposition team mates where actual bodily harm has been caused.

- Actual physical violence towards opponent.

- Incidents on the pitch leading to both coaches and supporters brawling on the pitch.

- A player was injured and the coach ran on and hit the ref and attacked the opposing physio trying to help injured player.

**3. What positive signs have you seen on touchlines?**

- We are always told to encourage from the touchline – this is done by reinforcing positive behaviour and positive play to the players whilst the game is in progress.

- Positive encouragement, good sportsmanship.

- A relaxed atmosphere.

- Helping and assisting injured players on both teams.

- Good coaching and information to players is what I like, we do not talk to players in possession only when we lose the ball.

- Respect barriers have shown to be an effective deterrent and encouraging parents to stand at the opposite side of the pitch ensures you as a coach have more control over the players when they are both on and off the pitch.

- Parents and coaches respecting the Respect campaign and the officials. Every club needs a code to protect both players and coaches.

## 4. What positive scenes have you seen on the field of play?

- I have witnessed during this season players encouraging one another whilst playing – being respectful to match officials.

- Encouragement to play fair - but this is usually with younger age groups.

- Usual good sportsmanship etc.

- Good sportsmanship.

- Fair play when tackled in penalty box, telling the ref about defenders touching ball and it not being a foul.

- Abuse towards referees has dropped to virtually none, which has seen more youngsters getting involved in the refereeing side as they no longer feel intimidated.

- As a Charter Standard Club with an official welfare officer, we implement all the standards and make sure all coaches/helpers are both trained and qualified to administer them.

## 5. Do you implement RESPECT into your coaching and if so, what have you changed about your coaching, groups and games ?

- In training, I am always encouraging positive play.

- Especially when in schools, I have to be aware that there is a wide range of ability within the group, so have to pitch the session at the right level.

- I am always encouraging players and pupils to discuss things during a session/lesson – this way the players have to listen and respect the thoughts of players in the group.

- Yes, my method and tone of communication.

- Always, it is an effective deterrent. Constant and consistent implementation of Respect rules has ensured impeccable behaviour from the sidelines at our games.

- I'm not as aggressive coaching and not commentary coaching anymore.

- I've tried to ask the people I coach and assist how my behaviour could change to help them develop as a player, if that would be physically, mentally, psychologically, tactical or technical.

- Players co-operating with officials - listening and putting things into practice without questioning.

**6. What have you installed in your club to deal with the perpetrators?**

- Action is taken and re-training etc.

- Parent contract and zero tolerance policy.

- I have not changed my coaching style, I have always installed respect and would not accept this from any player/pupil. I have tried to talk to the girls I coach about how this sort of behaviour and attitude is wrong for the game and if it happens I ban them from playing the next game.

- I've tried to ask the people I coach and assist how my behaviour could change to help them develop as a player, if that would be physically, mentally, psychologically, tactical or technical.

- We have a discipline procedure as part of the charter standards and our coaches are all trained to deal with incidents and report them back to the club where they are dealt with by the committee.

- They simply are asked to leave and find another club.

I sent a number of e-mails right across the board and received lots of replies with many interesting stories and opinions. I'm still receiving replies and hope that some of the information will feature in future editions of this book.

It seems wherever I look, someone has a story to tell. Andy Ripley, who is a PE teacher, has won the National Cup twice at school boy level as a coach; which is huge tribute to him and his school - Malet Lambert in Hull. He tells many a disturbing story about some of the teams that arrive at his school from all over the country.

One day a team came with one intention, which was simply to "FIGHT"; from the teachers with the team, to the captain and travelling fans. They knew they wouldn't win on the football pitch so set out to intimidate their opponents. Inexcusable behaviour.

An interesting reply came from York City who were happy to inform me that they had no problems with any of the above questions from any of their age groups. A brilliant, encouraging response and it is good that clubs can be proud to say that. Again, with future editions I would hope to add more clubs to the list.

## The FA and County FAs

I contacted every County FA in the country, again asking them questions. The response was not very forthcoming, though I put this down to the confidentiality of the matters and the worry of where the information was heading. I felt it was better not to pester each county official and let them decide for themselves. I hope, as I've already spoken about, that I can extend this piece further on future releases of the book and get more officials on board. I received this e-mail below from Helen Hever from the Essex FA which confirmed my conclusion that despite my attempts, I would have to feed off the national information I had found.

Good Afternoon Chris
Thank you for your email.
I can see that you have contacted various County FA's with the request to which I am sure you will see some different trends as all county's are different. I would like direct you to the
http://www.thefa.com/Leagues/Respect where the latest information can be found. There is also now Respect FC, which is the new football club

set up to recognise the programme.  The programme continues to evolve.

Essex has seen an improvement and together with safeguarding measures, poor behaviour can be monitored and addressed. I wish you well with your project.

Kind Regards
Helen Hever

The County FAs have all nominated Respect officers within their organisations, along with welfare officers, to monitor the progress made.

The FA's are pretty clear with their message and ensure everyone is on board. From June 2010 teams could not register with leagues without their club having a child welfare officer, and I'm sure given time the same will apply for the role of Respect officer within the club.

Alan Poulain from the Huntingdonshire FA gave me the kind of answers I was looking for, as he was very frank in his views and pulled no punches.

## 1. Has there been an Improvement since the attention within the media?

I think this will depend on which media source you look into. There are some very cynical reporters out there and whatever occurs on the field of play, they will tell you that Respect is not working. Locally however the media take a different view and report what they see and do not look for holes in differing campaigns.

On the whole I believe there has been a big difference but the media do not tend to report good news do they?

## 2. Do you feel the new FA directives will help with the RESPECT campaign?

Depends what you mean by new directives: the Respect FC initiative has had a lukewarm reception as it has not really been seen outside. There was supposed to be media coverage during the FA Cup 4th round games but I cannot say I saw very much. The website sign up has only attracted just under 17000 people. This has been running for over 6 weeks and I think we would have expected more.

## 3. What do you feel causes parents to react the way they do?

The facts of life are simple. The pressures on people to win at all costs extends beyond themselves to whoever they 'support'. Touchline behaviour means that it extends to their child and the referee who might stop their child or team 'winning'. Life is not so simple anymore, the aggression shown on the touchline is only the same aggression seen in everyday actions of people, road rage, cup cake rage (today's news) etc.

## 4. Hopes for the future?

We cannot give up on doing what we believe is right. If we carry on telling Youth clubs that winning is not everything, enjoyment and taking part mean so much more. Little and often is what I tell my clubs. But keep the pressure up and do not compromise.

How about an education course in refereeing for all match day commentators, not just the high profile guys.

Why not put the loud mouth parents through a coaching or referee course before they can rejoin the touchline, if challenged on behaviour.

**5. And what has your FA implemented to change things different from any other?**

We started our Touchline Respect Barriers before the expensive national FA barriers were launched. My Clubs are used to this and we also allow the white line approach, where the clubs also have a 'Don't X The Line' high viz vest supplied by Hunts FA. We are trying to keep the visibility at our matches high and try to encourage Respect this way.

## The Leagues

The city of Hull boasts one of the biggest leagues in England and is also a pioneer. The Hull Boys Sunday Football League (HBSFL) celebrated after becoming the first League in England to achieve the prestigious FA Charter Standard League award in 2009.

The Charter Standard League award is a flagship initiative by the FA and assesses the ability of a League to provide a high quality, safe and enjoyable football experience against a standard set of criteria. It also encourages the League to continually develop, through ongoing support from staff at the East Riding FA. Ongoing development is reviewed against a League Development Plan, as part of an annual health check process.

Quite fittingly, the League also celebrated its 50th anniversary in 2010 and is currently providing football for just under 6,000 players each week through its 416 member teams.

"I am delighted that the Hull Boys League was the first in England to achieve the Charter Standard League award," said Andrew Hailwood, The FA's Regional Football Development Manager (North). "It is testament to the commitment and progressive attitude of this League and its' member clubs that the League was able to come through this process in such a short space of time. Charter Standard League status is far more than a paper exercise," he continued. "It is a process through which a League and its clubs can look to improve their activities across a range of areas including, child protection, coaching, officiating and administration. Hull Boys League should be applauded for embracing this process and demonstrating that they are constantly striving to improve, for players, coaches, referees and clubs."

As part of the criteria to attain the League award, clubs have also had to become Charter Standard Clubs and therefore undertake some key areas of improvement in their operating standards. Each club must now have in place amongst other things, a Welfare Officer and a Child Protection Policy. All volunteers must have CRB checks and managers/coaches must have appropriate coaching, Safeguarding Children and Emergency Aid qualifications.

The Mitcham Little League has endorsed the Respect Campaign and it is always acknowledged prior to kick off. Every club skipper must wear their Respect arm band and they teach form a young age (12+) the importance of the role of the captain and why the particular player has been selected for this privilege. On one particular weekend prior to kick off, every team showed Respect toward the victims of the Japanese Earthquake. This is where football unites with the community. There are 1000s of great examples of unsung heroes who give their time every week. Although this is not in the press or promoted publicly, we all know great people who produce great results week in week out. They support all at grass roots level and will continue to always be Respectful towards all involved in this special sport.

Dermot Collins (the FAs Respect Manager) singled out the Northern Premier League as an example of good practice. The league keeps a close eye on the disciplinary stats of their teams – how they compare to each other and also against other teams in similar leagues. They then approach the club chairman or secretary with this information and quite often it's enough to then prompt the club to talk formally with the managers and players and in some cases invite referees into the club to discuss how additional cautions or dismissals can be avoided. The result of this effort can be seen in the fact that the level of cautions in the Northern Premier League has fallen by 30 % compared to the same period last season.

The end of year secretary's report for one league in the North East was brutal in its condemnation of verbal abuse towards referee's by parents and coaches. The clubs were reminded that the league was a Respect league and asked each club to take more responsibility. This has to stop, they clearly state, otherwise the club will be disciplined accordingly.

I spent some time researching the different regions and found that some leagues had already brought in the new directives and played 9 v 9 amongst other things. They had incorporated new ideas which not just followed the FA's instructions but also engineered new formats that reflected their own beliefs and ideas for their children.

*Good afternoon Lesley,*
*I have been researching the RESPECT campaign for a project I am currently working with. I was hoping you would answer these few questions for me?*
*I run a club myself in East Yorkshire, and know of the problems out there, and hoped you could help me with some questions? I am also looking for a view from the county FA's for the project.*

*I look forward to hearing from you,*
*Regards, Chris Kirkham*

I began with Lesley Allon from the Bolton Bury and District Junior Football League and asked him the following questions:

**1. Has there been an improvement since the attention within the media?**

At first there was a noticeable improvement which was encouraging. Now with a few teams we have to keep reminding them but on the whole the improved level is being maintained.

**2. Do you feel the new FA directives will help with the RESPECT campaign?**

Can't do any harm, but really feel that Respect has to be shown to apply throughout all levels of the game not just at grass roots.

**3. What do you feel causes parents to react the way they do?**

Who knows? If you manufactured a medicine to cure it you'd make a fortune.

**4. Hopes for the future?**

To persuade and educate everyone that what we are trying to implement is needed to preserve the integrity of this game we all enjoy.

Looking at many leagues throughout the country, most if not all are now Charter Standard and have the Respect campaign at the forefront of their websites.

The leagues are set for a change with the new directives as the plan to have less competitive games and the non publication of league tables becomes incorporated.

**"Without grass roots football the professional game would not exist and that is why it is so important for there to be respect and good behaviour at this level of the game, and indeed at every level"**

The above statement was taken from the Pin Point Recruitment Junior Football League who are delighted to be able to provide some high quality "endorsements" from both organisations who support what they do; and past players who recognise the impact the league had on their early careers.

Just to set the scene, the league was renamed the Pin Point Recruitment Junior Football League for the 2010-2011 season. Prior to this they were more affectionately known to everyone in grassroots football across the North East simply as the NABC League.

The league has the backing of all FA officials and from past players such as Newcastle's keeper Steve Harper, who endorses the league.

The Shropshire league became Charter standard in 2011 and has a motto that reads:

### "Ability is nothing without opportunity"

They offer an excellent structure to play and have worked very hard achieve their goals.

Members of Oldham's Junior Soccer League were invited to Oldham Athletics' Boundary Park pitch for a presentation when they gained Charter Standard status in May 2011. Members of the league, including those who have participated in it, were welcomed to the Oldham Athletic versus Charlton Athletic match. Each member of the league received complimentary tickets and was welcomed onto the pitch during half time to pick up the award. An excellent way to show both the leagues and local clubs are working together.

The Manchester FA recognised the great work being done by the league within the borough of Oldham. The league runs all types of innovative small sided football for the younger ages. The formats range from 3v3, 4v4 to mini soccer football. The formats used give all participants a greater opportunity to be involved in the game and looks to develop the players both individually and as part of a team. Much like in Spain.

The Sheffield and Hallamshire FA have Charter Standard Leagues which demonstrate that they are committed to the Respect programme and have procedures in place to improve standards. This is common trait amongst many of the FA's and leagues I researched and it is pleasing to be safe in the knowledge that everyone is simply on board with the matter.

By achieving Charter Standard status, a league will:
- Target investment
- Deliver an improved service and support structure to leagues
- Improve communication with leagues
- Ensure succession planning within leagues
- Rationalise existing league structures
- Help implement the principles of Long Term Player Development
- Grow football for underrepresented groups
- Improve efficiency and sustainability of leagues

The league will have a 6 point criteria as shown on the following page:

## Charter Standard League criteria

The criteria for the Programme are divided into 6 development areas, reflecting the approach of the National Game Strategy:

- Growth and Retention
- Raising Standards and Addressing Behaviour
- Better Players
- Running the Game
- Workforce Development
- All Goals and Enablers

And of course deliver the Respect Programme.

On the day the FA launched a new Respect initiative, Respect FC, The Halton and District Football league in Chesire invited Trevor Massey, the Cheshire FA Referee Development Officer and Respect lead speaker, to give a short presentation to all member clubs. The meeting held at the The Pavilions, Weston Point, was attended by the majority of clubs within the league. All clubs attending the event were issued with new Respect Codes of Conduct to be signed by all club officials, managers, players and spectators.

Any clubs that didn't attend the event were sent their new code of conduct packs directly. The leagues procedures were all in place and were geared up to the campaign. It is now the jobs of the clubs to fulfil the leagues aspirations, not letting them down, as the penalties could be very harsh. One moment of madness can ruin it for everybody.

The benefits to the leagues were clear and by signing up to working towards Charter Standard League status, leagues will be demonstrating that they are willing to work towards a minimum operating standard. This will help to raise standards and address poor behaviour within the league and member clubs will be encouraged to gain Charter Standard Club status as part of the Charter Standard League criteria. Leagues will also be demonstrating, by reviewing what they do well, what they want to do better and by identifying how they can improve, that they are committed to developing better players and to investing in the workforce. The benefits of achieving Charter Standard League status are that leagues will have a clear development plan in place, together with an agreed support package with their County FA. Charter Standard Leagues will also be demonstrating that they are committed to the Respect programme and will have procedures in place to improve standards and address poor behaviour in the game, a key priority for all those involved in football. Leagues will also gain recognition that they are committed to a quality experience for all and that they are a well run league.

Broadly speaking, the leagues are all on board with the Respect campaign none more so than the Chad Mansfield Youth Football League, who on their website issue this rallying cry...

### It's not a campaign
### It's more than a slogan
### It's a long term commitment
### Lose respect, lose the game

The English Premier League is now part of a global game that has become bigger and brighter than ever envisaged. The pressure on the match officials is more a focal point than ever before. Major incidents send shockwaves through the game. There has to be a happy medium and at grassroots, the referee must be given the support from the club, without be hounded out by parents like a pack of vultures or the paparazzi!

## The Grassroots Show...

In my view, the Grassroots Show is a must for any coach, secretary or club representative out there. Every year at the beginning of June, from the Friday of half term to the Sunday, a superb show of coaching displays and demonstrations takes place at the NEC in Birmingham. There are also guest speakers talking about all elements of the game; from a glorious goal, cross or pass; to the Respect campaign. At the show there are many stalls that help your club build up a directory of contacts and also a chance to meet and sign up to the Don't X the Line campaign.

Coaches such as Chris Coleman, Razor Ruddock, Ian Hollaway, Iain Dowie and Peter Taylor were also in attendance, along with Graham Taylor who is the ambassador for the show.

There are some fantastic stalls with a wealth of information for your club, whether you are buying a new football, new kit or looking at fundraising ideas, or administration.

With loads of famous faces in attendance throughout the three days, it was a chance to meet some of the big names in football – including Robbie Savage and Dion Dublin. There was a long list of football pro's who run technical sessions, take part in panel discussions and answer questions in open Q&A sessions.

Some of the highlights of 2011 show included:

- The opportunity to watch some of the top football coaches run their own innovative sessions in the Precision Training Coaching and Goalkeeping Arena.
- Meeting famous celebrities.
- Watching, listening to and interacting with some of the biggest names in the professional game.
- Finding out about the latest trends in the world of football from the 90+ exhibitors on the exhibition floor.

- Watching the world's leading freestyler Billy Wingrove showcase his skills.

For more information, go to their website:
www.grassrootsfootball.com

## Listening to Graham Taylor

As the Grassroots show in June 2011 reached its climax, I sat down and listened to Graham Taylor. Despite once being the England boss, he is unfortunately probably better remembered for his "do I not like that" statement, after a 1993 fly-on-the-wall documentary on Channel 4 amazed the world of football. Following his stint with England and spells back at Aston Villa and Watford, he now works as a respected media pundit and ambassador for the Grassroots show.

Taylor began by sharing his feelings on the subject of parents on the touchline. His verdict was one already voiced several times in this book: "This is something that really irritates me and I choose to watch my Grandchild play from a distance."

He also spoke intelligently about the issues facing the parent-coach. Having had to pay subscription fees for pitches, kit and the like, the FA also insist on coaches paying for qualifications. "How can coaches become better qualified if it is going to cost not only a fortune but time off work?" he asked. It could cost a coach thousands of pounds to reach a higher standard. Can coaches afford this? And does this give everyone equal access to qualifications or will financial barriers create a glass ceiling?

Taylor believes a Level One coaching course should be free and this would help clubs have more coaches and give parents a better understanding of the game. He sees areas of football stagnating and perceives very little change in 20 years at International level. Taylor also feels that since the arrival of 43 academies, there has been the same success rate for young footballers as before academies were set up. Graham explained that the next generation need to take over from the men in suits and the likes of Alan Shearer and co's input could be valuable. He welcomed the arrival of Gareth Southgate to the FA. Praising Wales and Scotland, he remained baffled why these tiny counterparts in the context of the global game are miles ahead of England at grassroots.

Through my own research and experience, these nations seem to make life easier for coaches and incorporate things quicker into their game, rather than to wait around forever.

Taylor rounded up the conversation with the fact he deliberately doesn't get involved with his Grandson's football and just wants him to enjoy it with a smile on his face along with the millions of young players out there.

Graham is very passionate about the state of the English game and often speaks in seminars about the influence of parents on their child's footballing life. Since the aforementioned The Impossible Dream documentary, he has seen a lot of football but not enough to make him feel that enough has been done to help those at grassroots level. I'm sure many will argue and disagree with his points, though the beauty of the game is the difference in opinions.

# PART FOUR

## Respect FC

 "Respect FC, the club with one goal – to rid the game of the gobby morons." Mark Watson

January 2011 saw the birth of a new "virtual" football club aptly named Respect FC. The Football Association took a radical new approach to tackling bad behaviour from fans and players and decided to launch its own football club. However, the club only exists online, with a stated aim not of winning matches but of uniting fans against the ugly side of the beautiful game; creating a safe and enjoyable environment in which football can take place and using a website to promote the club amongst junior soccer clubs from all counties.

Comedian and avid Bristol City fan Mark Watson was appointed as Chairman and instantly filmed an impassioned plea from the club's modest headquarters, which features starring roles from former Liverpool captain Neil 'Razor' Ruddock, Portsmouth legend Steve Claridge and Sky Sports commentator Chris Kamara. Robbie Savage, a player with a record of dissent against referees, signed up a few days after the launch.

On signing for Respect FC, Savage said on www.sport.co.uk website:

"I'm sure many people will be surprised by my latest move, and I know I may not have set the most shining example in the past, but I've come to realise that poor behaviour is not an acceptable part of football – be it on the pitches, in the stands or even down the local park. My two sons both enjoy the game and it's my responsibility as their dad to make sure that the environment in which they are playing or watching football is a safe and respectable one. I've looked at my own behaviour, now I'm asking others to do the same and join me in supporting Respect FC."

Bold statements from a player who has enjoyed a colourful career, playing for Crewe Alexandra, Manchester United, Leicester City, Birmingham City, Blackburn Rovers and Derby County before retiring in May 2011. Notably, he even managed to collect a booking as he skippered Derby County for he last time away at Reading.

He gained notoriety for his playing style; in particular, his combative midfield play and gesticulating that tended to wind up both opposition players and fans. In 2008, the Daily Mail labelled him as the dirtiest player in Premier League history, based on numbers of yellow cards received, though he has since lost his "record" to Lee Bowyer. Robbie writes a regular column for the Daily Mirror, who describe him as "love him or hate him, he's marmite!"

Respect FC was not be your usual football club; it's a football club made up of people from all walks of life, with one collective goal – to bring Respect back to the game we all love. For every fan that joins Respect FC, The FA has pledged to put £1 back into the Respect initiative within grassroots football up to the value of £50k. Six months after the launch, the balance raised stood at £19k; a significant amount but still less than half of the allotted money. Members of the Club will be able to vote online at www.RespectFootballClub.com to say how this money is used at the end of the 2010-11 season (the range of options includes pitch side barriers or Respect Awards).

Respect FC is not just about raising awareness; it's much more than that. Everyone who is involved in the game in some way is aware of poor behaviour and knows that – be it towards referees, players or fellow fans – it is wrong. The challenge now is to unite, change people's attitudes and make people realise that verbal and physical abuse are not acceptable in the game.

Watson said on the Respect F.C website "We know that it's so much easier to take a stand against poor behaviour if you are not on your own, if you have someone else on your team. Collectively we can stand up to the gobby morons. If you'd like to show the people spoiling our game, what they're up against go to RespectFootballClub.com to join my new football club, Respect FC, the club with one goal – to rid the game of the gobby morons."

Alex Horne, FA General Secretary, added on the site:

**"Football fans from all clubs and all leagues have a collective responsibility to let others know that they will not stand for this behaviour from the grassroots of the game up to the international stage. That's why we're asking everyone, to ask everyone, to join the club and together win the match against bad behaviour."**

Fans are encouraged to log onto www.RespectFootballClub.com and register their support to unite against the ugly side of football.

# Sale United

*(includes extracts from the Sale United website)*

Sale United FC achieved the FA Charter Standard in 2002 and became Charter Standard Development Club of the Year 2010. Sale United are proud of their reputation that children who are involved with the Club receive a quality experience that stretches beyond just football. Families "belong" to the Club so much so that second generation players are now playing for [Manchester] United. Coaches evolve through the ranks which builds a family feeling at the Club. Their Zero Tolerance policy has been recognised nationally and is the envy of many.

Sale United's even stage an annual tour of Holland for the Under 13s which is described as "an educational adventure and an experience the children will never forget". The Club is also groundbreaking in developing different aspects of football, including Age Appropriate Coaching and its latest achievement is "Power Chair football*."

*\*Power Chair Football, also known as Power Soccer is a competitive team sport for people with disabilities who use their own power wheelchairs.*

Sale United are a great example to other clubs so I thought it would be useful to include more information about their groundbreaking Zero Tolerance policy.

## Zero Tolerance

Sickened by the rising levels of abuse towards officials, parents and players, Sale United hit back with a very successful Zero Tolerance campaign that my club have now adopted. Searching the internet, I found that many others have followed suit.

One of the original driving forces in what was to become the Respect movement was Total Youth Football, a monthly magazine designed to help coaches. It produced session plans, along with other good sections to provide advice and help to those running football teams. The magazine was brilliant in every way but sadly it went into liquidation in Summer 2008. Total Youth Football reported on some of the issues affecting our game at grassroots level and decided to do something about it. The magazine worked with Sale United to produce an A4 template designed for clubs to laminate and hand out before games (a copy is included in this chapter). A copy can be also be found on my website for you to use and all you need to do is enter your own clubs details.

The Sale United Chairman, Colin Dowdy, was interviewed and he began by telling us: "Cars were getting attacked, parents were being abused and managers having to physically protect their teams from people on the touchline "

His club had 80 volunteer coaches, all at least Level One FA Coaches, with over 500 players and 40 teams. This is some achievement when I look at my own club boasting just 5 teams. Poor Colin has the problems I endure multiplied by eight!

He described it as an ugly problem which has plagued this family club, a stones throw from Manchester United Football Club. It was hard to imagine that this club would have problems with its excellent voluntary brigade and any shameful behaviour must have been embarrassing whilst also endangering everything the club was trying hard to achieve.

At first glance, Sale United are like any other big junior club and it was hard to see how any problems could possibly occur with such a strong foundation. It was around 2003 when they took it upon themselves to design a discipline procedure as they found growing problems at mini soccer; the setting for an alarming number of incidents in this book. They found that some parents were unwilling to re-enrol their children unless something was done as some of the behaviour was getting out of control. One example, which Colin shared with Total Football, described how one young player chased another lad around the pitch and eventually got him to the floor and delivered a string of Rocky style punches. The referee stepped in and the perpetrator turned out to be the manager's son. The Manager showed no remorse and asked what the problem was, as its part of the game and only football!

This prompted the club to take action. Having had recent incidents where police had to be called on for assault charges, the club had little option but to address the problems.

Colin's grandson was also a local referee who came back with many a tale, including one day when an eight year old had given him a torrent of abuse, using words he should not have known existed!

Colin felt both kids and parents wound each other up and the kids in particular never really knew how to behave. Again Colin referred to the influence of TV and stars of the Premier League who exhibit behaviour that kids go out and replicate.

When I coach myself I refer to players the kids can relate to, which was easy in the days of Micheal Owen at his peak and David Beckham, though I struggle nowadays.

With all the parental mayhem and behaviour of young players, which had sunk to new depths, they decided on a plan of attack. Sale produced a basic card stating that they would not tolerate this sort of anti-social behaviour. They were well aware the code of conduct was in use and wanted to target the sideline directly on match day.

You may wish to use something similar if you are involved in youth football.

The card gave the power back to Sale United and with clear simple rules printed on it, the card empowered club officials and gave them the chance to ask the perpetrators to leave the field or sideline for contravening written regulations. Sale United felt responsible for their spectators and felt it necessary to make it a safe and friendly environment for the visiting team. They took the idea to their league which was met with a great response from clubs and Zero Tolerance on the touchlines was born.

The introduction of the card had fast and positive results as less parental abuse was reported along with a significant decline in cautions being issued. The parents stopped yelling and screaming. They stopped getting wound up and their tempers simmered down. The coaches were more relaxed as they could actually coach and not be in confrontations with Mad Max the parent.

The scheme made the front page of the Manchester Evening News. Media interest grew and the FA showcased the scheme at a seminar fronted by Sir Trevor Brooking and Sir Geoff Hurst.

The Cheshire FA reported in June 2010 that this policy was the envy of others and won the FA Charter Standard Club of the Year.

Example of a Sale United matchday card

## INAPPROPRIATE LANGUAGE & REFEREE ABUSE

_____F.C acknowledges that every child, young person or adult who plays or participates in football, should be able to take part in an enjoyable and safe environment, and be protected from poor practice and abuse.

_____Football Club will not tolerate inappropriate language or threatening behaviour used on match sidelines, particularly verbal or physical abuse directed at Match Officials.

Match Officials are just as entitled to enjoy the match as players and spectators.

_____ reserve the right to ask anyone demonstrating actions deemed to conflict with Club policy to move away from the match sidelines.

Spectators please stand behind the barriers at all times
Coaches have an area at the opposite side of the pitch
Your co-operation is very much appreciated.

# Don't X The Line campaign

Mal Lee has been one of the main pioneers of the Respect campaign in the UK. I met Mal at the Grassroots show in Birmingham in 2008 and found his plans, stories and most of all his ambition to fight the problems on the touchline inspiring. I have continued to follow his work since. At the time, I signed our club up to his campaign and purchased barriers from him, along with obtaining some stickers and badges for the club. My own club, The Burlington Jackdaws, were formed in 2006, so had a huge advantage as the new initiatives were adopted ahead of their time. I imagine for some clubs more set in their ways, trying to change people and introduce new ideas may have been more difficult.

Mal says on his website that the reason he got behind this project was that the changing face of grass roots football has been a major worry over the past five years and much of this has come from pushy parents and glory seeking managers/coaches. The touchlines at our junior leagues have become a breeding ground for verbal abuse, mainly directed at referees. Some of these pushy parents feel that they have to show their aggression and anger in front of the children. Do they realise what sort of message they are sending out these children; the future of our country? One thing they must realise is that their children, first and foremost, look up to them and see them as role models. What the children see they copy, what the children hear they repeat, so if mum or dad are hurling abuse at the referee they then believe it is okay for them to do the same.

Mal has been working with volunteers over the last five years with the 'Don't X the Line Campaign' to eradicate aggressive and abusive behaviour by parents and make them aware that showing respect and sportsmanship on and off the field is the key for good behaviour. The campaign has been a success; it works and has been adopted all over this country and beyond.

A major problem was pitch encroachment. He witnessed quite a few incidents over the years. Sometimes parents were that far on the pitch it was hard for the goalkeepers to see what was going on in the games! How do we combat that? The methods are so simple; you segregate the supporters (usually parents) of each team, if possible on opposite touchlines. If that is not possible, split the one touchline into two for each set of parents/supporters. No parents/spectators are allowed to stand behind the goals. This makes it easier for the referee and/or committees to pinpoint which club the verbal abuse is directed from and they can then act accordingly. There needed to be some easy way to segregate people. Mal said "I noticed that when cones were used in games people walked over them and ended up back on the pitch rather than stretching their necks to see when a person steps in front blocking the view. I always wanted some kind of barrier. I felt this was the only way to really combat the problems. If a barrier was used, it would act as a massive deterrent, especially for pitch encroachment."

Mal used the Respect Zone barriers with the Don't X the Line Campaign at tournaments, with excellent results and glowing reports from the Referees, League Committees and, yes, the parents/spectators. The children could actually pick the ball up when it went out for a throw-in without getting lost in between legs and bodies.

## In praise of Don't X The Line...

"There is no doubt that the DXTL campaign has helped the FA to boost the recruitment and retention figures of match officials around the UK. I hope that club and league officials will join us in this campaign to improve the image of the game. I can assure you that if you put in a call or email to Mal Lee you will be greeted with great enthusiasm. DONT X THE

LINE is supported by past and current Premier League Referees Thank you for your support"
*Keith Hackett, Premier League Referee Ambassador, Don't X the Line Ambassador*

"Improving the standards of touchline behaviour at grassroots level can only encourage more children and young Referee's to get involved and participate in the game we all love. We at the PGMOL are pleased to support the campaign, as their effort and commitment will only reward the future of our game and achieve positive results at every Level."
*Mike Riley-General Manager PGMOL (Professional Game Match Officials Limited)*

"It is an honour to be asked to be an ambassador for the Don't X the Line, I obviously started myself at grassroots level and I do understand the problem we have with referees and youngsters becoming increasingly under pressure from a minority of pushy spectators whilst participating in grassroots football"
*Jamie Carragher, Liverpool FC*

"I was delighted to see Malcolm Lee presented with the inaugural Bobby Moore Award for his amazing contribution to the game in his native Merseyside. The passion he's shown for grassroots football over the last 20 years is truly inspiring. Bobby would have been so honoured to see The FA recognising someone like Malcolm in this way, and proud to have it done in his name."
*Stephanie Moore MBE, patron of the Bobby Moore Fund for Cancer Research UK*

# Keep it Shut survey

Total Youth Football magazine really homed in the touchline abuse, and launched their own campaign "KEEP IT SHUT". They embarked on producing a survey that would highlight the areas that most needed care and attention. They were simply inundated with responses, stories, ideas and suggestions.

Their mission was to highlight and tackle all forms of abuse in youth football. What follows is a breakdown of the information, which acknowledged the incredible feedback and which the magazine made clear would be passed onto the relevant football authorities in the UK.

575 surveys were filled in and returned from all over the UK. 511 respondents were men and 64 women. The average age of the respondents was 40. 184 classed themselves as coaches and 183 were team managers. 113 referees also responded.

The first question asked was:

## Have you witnessed any abuse from parents and spectators?

A staggering 475 replied that they had experienced bad behaviour on the touchline. 83% recording unacceptable verbal abuse or interference from parents and spectators at a youth football match in which their own child had been involved in. 468 (82%) reported that they had also seen similar actions aimed at officials.

A very concerning 21%, a fifth of the survey, highlighted the worrying physical violence they had seen relating to youth football. 84% pointed the finger at the current crop of professional players.

Amazingly, only 4% had put they had not seen any problems along these lines at junior soccer.

The positives signs were that clubs were dealing with problems on and off the pitch and were happy to record this. Though it was clear from the evidence provided from the survey that there was a real problem at youth level with abuse and all looked to their county FA's for more support for clubs in this area.

The prayers of many clubs have been answered since the campaign with clubs having to appoint a Child Welfare Officer and all having to be Charter Standard.

"Keep it Shut" issued badges and Total Youth Football kept readers up to date with developments to hopefully (in their words) "To help you rid all forms of abuse from your pitches and touchlines".

## Women's Football

A few decades ago, the involvement of women in football was minimal; a tea lady or young girl selling lottery tickets who would be subjected to all manner of vulgar chants as she walked around the pitch. Thankfully, times have changed. Women have since entered the boardroom, make up a higher proportion of the crowd and participation in the women's game has grown to the point where big games can attract in excess of 20,000 spectators. Gender is no barrier to learning and implementing the rules of the game and female referees and assistant referees can now been seen at all levels of the game, including the Premier League.

**Unfortunately, the acceptance of women officials has been slow in some quarters and is an area of football where a distinct lack of respect can be found.**

One of the most high profile examples of this came when supposedly "off air" comments by two Sky TV pundits were reported. Anyone who followed football knew exactly who Richard Keys and Andy Gray were. In January 2011, those that didn't were made aware of the pair who had graced our screens as the face of Sky Sports Premier League coverage for 20 years, as their comments regarding a female referee made front page and headline news.

Ahead of a live Saturday lunch time game at Wolverhampton Wanders, Assistant Referee Sian Massey found herself at the centre of a scandal after the two Sky Sports presenters made sexist remarks about her which would see the double act removed from our screens.

Andy Gray had a fantastic football career, playing for clubs both north and south of the border, as well as representing Scotland 20 times scoring 7 goals. In 1978 he made history when he was awarded the PFA Young Player of the Year and PFA Players' Player of the Year award in the same year (a historic double not repeated until Cristiano Ronaldo won both awards 30 years later). At the time he was the youngest player to earn the Players' Player of the Year award, and the first player to win more than one of the official three Player of the Year awards in the same season. He went on to be a successful co-commentator with Sky and now continues his work with Talksport

Richard Keys began his TV career in the 80s, co-presenting TV-am, a breakfast show on the ITV network, with Anne Diamond. He also commentated on football matches for ITV. Keys was one of the presenters for The Sports Channel on British Satellite Broadcasting (BSB) in Spring 1990. When BSB merged with Sky in 1991, the channel was renamed Sky Sports. Keys presented TV-am for the final time on 28 December 1990 before he left for Sky Sports full time.

In January 2011, Keys and his colleague Andy Gray were suspended for off-air remarks they made about a Sian Massey; he resigned on 26 January, subsequent to Gray's dismissal and now works with Gray on Talksport on a credible morning show from 10am-1pm. Sky Sports has said off-air remarks made by two football presenters about female assistant referee Sian Massey were "not acceptable". Believing their microphones were off, the pair agreed female officials "don't know the offside rule". In a statement, Sky said the two men had apologised for the comments.

The media reported...

"The Football Association gave its support to Ms Massey, 25, who made a correct borderline call in the build-up to Liverpool's first goal at the Molineux stadium in Wolverhampton.

Speaking ahead of the match, Mr Keys said "somebody better get down there and explain offside to her" and Mr Gray remarked "women don't know the offside rule". Mr Keys then said "of course they don't", before adding: "I can guarantee you there'll be a big one today. [Liverpool manager] Kenny [Dalglish] will go potty."

He then went on to remark on comments made by West Ham vice-chairman Karren Brady in the Sun newspaper on that fateful Saturday morning about the level of sexism in football. "See charming Karren Brady this morning complaining about sexism? Yeah. Do me a favour, love," he said.

Sky said: "The comments are not acceptable. They were not made on air but we have spoken to Richard and Andy and told them our views and they have apologised and expressed their regret."

Sky said and did what was expected of them in such circumstances but Sky Sports may also wish to consider their own role in this. Female co-presenters on Sky are almost always significantly younger than their male counterparts (sometimes by a couple of decades) and glamorously presented, rather than wrapped in a sheepskin at

Preston on a Tuesday night. It doesn't exactly challenge the stereotypes that underpinned Keys' and Gray's comments.

Days after this came a story that mirrored the national story with a club in the North Riding. The story reports on abuse directed towards a female referee but is also a useful case study to see how the FA Charter Standard can be used in addressing such problems.

The media reported:

"A girl - who was refereeing a cup match at the time - was described as being "absolutely tortured" after making some unpopular decisions. "There was hell on," said one spectator. "She was absolutely distraught." The same female referee was also abused during a match in 2009 for which the club was fined £150.

A spokesman said the club, Marton FC, would no longer tolerate verbal abuse, inappropriate comments or threats made by supporters, including racist or sexist jibes. Those found to do so could face lifetime bans, he added:

"It is bad enough for us to put our foot down. Over the years it has got worse and it's time to nip it in the bud. We are looking at safeguarding children. The aim is to allow our young people to play football in a friendly atmosphere and safe surroundings. However, this can be compromised by the ignorant few who sound off verbally, usually negative responses towards referees and their decision-making. It is verbal abuse, inappropriate comments or gestures, threats to maybe give the referee a good kicking' or 'break his legs'. Marton FC have now put in place marshals who will monitor all our games. If there are any problems we will ask people to leave. We need to nip it in the bud."

Marton FC has helped launch the careers of a number of players including David Wheater, Jonathan Woodgate, Stewart Downing, Lee Cattermole and Matthew Bates. But the club's reputation is being tarnished by a mindless minority, it says. They also reported that an eight year-old had been verbally abused by parents on the sidelines during an under-nines match.

The club's secretary, Mike Fairburn, said the incident involving the female referee was "awful". "It wasn't sexist abuse as such, but they were shouting and swearing at her and saying she didn't have a clue what she was doing," he said. "If we don't get charter status back then our 26 teams and 350 kids will be sent on their way and the club will have to close."

*(A fine example of the purpose and power of the FA Charter Standard)*

A spokesman for The FA said: "Marton FC need FA Charter Standard status to play in the Teeside Junior Football Alliance next season although this is not an absolute requirement for playing affiliated football elsewhere in North Riding. However, FA Charter Standard status is a fantastic accolade that all grassroots football clubs aspire to and the North Riding County FA has offered a number of measures that will support Marton FC in re-educating some of the people within their set up. Both North Riding County FA and Marton FC are committed to getting the Charter Standard suspension lifted."

After the reported incidents the club decided to recruit marshals to patrol the sidelines, in an attempt to control the behaviour on the touchlines.

## Codes of Conduct

A Code of Conduct should be issued to all parents along with parents and players when they sign up to a team. The code of conduct can be different for each club though is guided by the FA's code of conduct, which can be found on the FA website, and is usually included in league documents and clubs websites. Here is an example of one Burlington Jackdaws have used in the past; Please feel free to use and implement into your club:

# CODE OF CONDUCT FOR PLAYERS

_____FC's Code of Conduct for Players

Players are the most important people in sport. Playing for the team, and for the team to play well, is the most fundamental part of the game, but not winning at any costs.
Fair Play and respect for all others in the game is equally important.

All players of _____FC are expected to:

- Not to swear or use inappropriate or abusive language.
- To show due respect towards Match Officials, accept their decisions without protest and avoid words or actions which may mislead them.
- To show due respect for their opponents at all times, irrespective of the result of the game, and avoid violence and rough play.
- To accept success and failure, victory and defeat, equally.
- To abide by the instructions of their Coach and Team Officials, provided they do not contradict the spirit of this Code.
- To know and abide by the Laws, rules and spirit of the game.
- To give maximum effort and strive for the best possible performance during a game, whatever the current status of that game.
- To make every effort consistent with Fair Play and the Laws of the Game to help their own team PLAY WELL.
- To set a positive example to others, particularly younger players.
- No negative comments from players will be tolerated.

The players conduct is paramount to everything the clubs try to achieve. Despite the bad language they may hear on the TV from the professionals and the abuse they hear from the crowd, players are asked as individuals not to use inappropriate language on the field of play. They are asked to show respect to referee's and avoid influencing their decisions. Respect the opposition whether the score is 9-0 either way, or is a close encounter. The players must also accept the result and learn to accept the outcome. Coaches must set a good example so the players can adhere to their instructions. An understanding of the game (whether built up from playing, watching Match of The Day or playing "FIFA" on the Xbox) needs to be accompanied by understanding the spirit of the game. The player must follow fair play at all times and set examples to others. Many clubs recognise the importance of a good example and work heavily on recruiting older players within their system, to help coach the new generation coming through the ranks.

It is important that each member receives a code of conduct and signs a register of acceptance, giving the club the backing if anything should occur. It's also important if you are the parent or player to protect yourselves and knowing the ground rules. A code of conduct might end up stuck on the fridge door, sat in the car, or even discarded as rubbish at the start of the season. Whatever its destination, it is important that a contract of behaviour has been established and can then be referred to when needs be.

A code of conduct is in every classroom at school and every workplace. The document is familiar with in walks of life. It has to be understood by the players, or else you are asking for problems!

The parents and spectator's code of conduct is blunt in many respects and has had to be modified during the years due to the problems that arose.

The document asks the observer to simply watch and enjoy the game without any reaction other than applauding good play. The bottom line is - the behaviour is different to that of a spectator at high profile game where the stakes are high.

# CODE OF CONDUCT FOR PARENTS & SPECTATORS

_____ FC's Code of Conduct for Parents

Parents and spectators have a great influence on children's enjoyment and success in football. All children play football because they first and foremost enjoy the game – its fun.
Children enjoying football. Please stand behind the barriers at all times and let them enjoy it!

- Not to use foul or abusive/racist language in any circumstances.
- To always be positive and encouraging towards all players from both teams (not just your own child or the most talented), in a sensible and constructive manner.
- To avoid yelling at or ridiculing a child for making a mistake.
- To remember that children play football for their own enjoyment, not for your own entertainment.
- To show respect for the Match Officials.
- To accept defeat sensibly and with dignity and to encourage the children to do the same.
- To avoid coaching the children during the game.
- To accept the decisions and instructions of the Coach and other Team Officials - Remember, they are volunteers who give up their time and resources to provide football for your children.
- To abide by the Laws, rules and spirit of the game of football.
- To support all efforts to remove verbal and physical abuse from children's football and to promote this Code of Conduct amongst other Parents and Spectators.
- No Negative comments will be tolerated.

# PART FIVE

### Everything Changes Take That - 2003

## My Story Reprise III

The coaching, organising and operating of the football clubs and sessions have always been high on my agenda. Watching a player develop from picking daisies to a junior football team is as rewarding as the transition from junior club to school of excellences or academies. Working alongside coaches who advance to greater heights can also be worth being in the game for.

The aggression shown and demonstrated on touchlines on a whole sent a shudder down my spine and gave me one too many sleepless nights. Why be involved, and what do these parents exactly want?

Society has changed immensely with safeguarding your own child becoming a high priority with the exposure of the threat out there. No longer were children been dropped off to play, while mum and dad took the hour to go to the supermarket, the increasing support was building, which in many cases is a good thing. Though I do know players, now older, who despised their parents watching. Some youngsters now wince as their elders roll up, as their expectations are so high. A whistle here, a shout there, the player forgets his coaches instructions and listens to their parent. Why shouldn't they, after all, it is drilled in to them at home to respect both mother and father so, if they tell them to get out wide, why wouldn't they?

Some people will never change and will always blame the coach or the team. These are the same parents who will not offer to help out on match days or referee their child's game, with a shake of the head, a bad back or the wrong shoes on. On one occasion, one dad declined claiming to be completely ignorant of the rules. This seemed extremely odd, as he turned up week in week out to watch his son play and seemed to have an opinion on everything about the game!

I now feel that after beating (I felt) my head against a brick wall, there is no room for bad practice or bad behaviour on the touchlines. Everyone is on board and society will always have its flaws, and lack of secrets as super injunctions fall flat on their faces. The stories will still emerge and they may feel insignificant at the time but can be propelled by the power of the media or even be filmed for an embarrassing YouTube viewing. Big brother is always there, watching every move. Our football club are happy to be playing in a safe, friendly local area and have achieved many recent accolades. We strive for excellence (which our motto states) and through our experience together this can be achieved.

Many clubs will have tried new tricks to improve Respect and together we salute their work, on and off the pitch. The Respect campaign on launch could be seen as simple black and white instructions, with many grey areas according to interpretation. These areas are now nearing a colour because of the work of the clubs. I have fished around all aspects of the game for answers in the production of this work and in June 2011 I felt I reached a climax. The FA and media have analysed every part of the kids game and after Manchester United were comprehensively beaten by Barcelona in the Champions League final 2011, Sir Alex claimed the Catalan model was one we should learn from: "Kids there learn better than ours..." he said. More on this later.

Junior football has to become a more pleasurable experience, for coaches, parents, children, referees, onlookers and all those volunteers all over the country. I hope through my work, it will breathe more understanding into how the problems can dealt with and solved.

Who is to blame for this messy situation? The stories tell of stars giving young players no role models, or is it the parents themselves searching too hard for the reward? Or is it simply just the players: instructed by the coach to do this and that; with the additional stress of competition and the worry of failure? Is it the modern upbringing or the society of today? Or is it the coaches fault, as he gives up his time voluntarily, to do what I would describe as quite simply the hardest job in football. We can all pick the England team, but could we really do it? We are now all football managers: all over the country we are expert tacticians after playing FIFA or Pro Evolution Soccer; from reading the newspapers, listening to Talksport or watching Sky Sports News 24/7?

The list is endless, though within the stories, the full episode has been exposed. It has been brilliant to write and chat with different people about their views, even if not face to face but with the benefits of email and the internet.

The story is not over for me personally and I hope I can achieve further success in other areas of the game. The next step on my journey follows, with the 2011-12 season looking at the future of the youth game and the higher statesmen in the Premier league being more heavily monitored - the bar is set to be raised again.

## How do Children Learn Respect?

The next section focuses on how children perceive Respect. It is difficult, with children all over the country having different upbringings and education. One child may have paid private education, with no financial worries ever. Another may be in a large family, scrimping for every penny they get and see mum and dad split up. Working in a Christian academy, I researched the academies ethos and principles. With religious belief high on the agenda, the academy operates in a less than affluent area yet respect is still instilled into all children.

*They learn through observation.* They learn how to honour their parents by observing how their parents honour them and by seeing how their parents treat their grandparents. They learn how to honour government by observing how their parents respect the laws. They learn how to honour their employers by observing how their parents honour theirs and, they may learn to honour God by observing their parents do the same.

*Children learn through instruction.* Parents have a duty to behave and a duty to their children to instruct them in the reasons for being respectful. These principles equip children for success in life and prepare them to assume their place in life. Parents harm their children by not instructing and re-enforcing these truths.

## Being Respected

We observe early in life that if certain individuals are respected, it is assumed they are respectable. One of the difficult lessons to learn in life is that we are sometimes disappointed by those whom we have come to respect.

Sometimes the young demand respect for themselves. They are certainly entitled to the same honour which others receive. However, the same assumptions hold for them as well, those honoured are honourable and the respected are respected. If we want to be respected we must learn it and earn it.

Let us not wallow in the valley of despair, I say to you today my friends. And so even though we face the difficulties of today and tomorrow, let's still have a dream. It is a dream deeply rooted in the junior football dream.

## I have a dream...

I have a dream that one day this nation will rise up and live out the true meaning of its children and we hold these truths to be self-evident, that all men and women are created equal.

I have a dream that one day on all the playing fields in the UK, the sons and daughters of all the parents on show will be able to sit down together at the table of junior football.

I have a dream that one day the referees will be treated with utmost respect, with the state of the game sweltering with the heat of injustice, sweltering with the heat of abuse, and will be transformed into an oasis of freedom and enjoyment.

I have a dream that all young footballers will one day live in a nation where they will not be judged by their ability to play football of but by the content of their character.

I have a dream today!

Ok I'm not Martin Luther King, but it was laugh writing this bit!

## The Future of Children's Football

*(Contains excerpts of FA literature)*

Over the first few months of 2011 we have seen much discussion and dialogue at coaching meetings, League and County FA meetings and most importantly with children, to culminate in the principles of the Youth Development review.

The complete Youth Development Review and the 25 recommendations that have been put forward focus on three areas (whole game player development, coaching and international team development) but this consultation process will focus on the key matters around whole game young player development and three vital areas of improvement.

The recommendations have been made on one determining factor:

**If this is better for the child that plays the game then it has to be considered.**

Many adult values are very different from children's views and values and it is the latter that should drive our young player development system, not the former. It is wholly recognised that the financial situation of the country means that the Football Association have to be realistic about what they are proposing, yet it also needs to be inspirational. If there are hurdles and challenges to be overcome then the football family needs to work together to achieve these, ensuring that we create the best possible opportunity and environment for young people to play, enjoy and learn the game of football.

There were a series of 'Your Kids, Your Say' events, with 16 taking place around the country. They were an opportunity for grassroots volunteers to come and hear the proposals being put forward and then discuss the implications of these in-depth. There was also an opportunity to ask questions of key Football Association staff on the night and seek help and advice on overcoming some local challenges people had.

Children's football in England needs to be based on common sense, be exciting and innovative and be world-leading. We have a fantastic opportunity to be at the forefront of change and whilst not forgetting the excellent work that the army of volunteers and parents do for children across the country, ensure that we all pull together in the same direction.

This is the time to have your positive input to try and develop the game, taking it into a new era and moving it forward for young people, as their lives move forward at an unprecedented pace not experienced before. This is the time to evolve and embrace development and discuss some of the matters being raised.

After losing the Champions league final in 2011 at Wembley against Barcelona, Man United paraded their 19th Premier League trophy around Manchester. Sir Alex was asked many questions on the open top bus, and probably most popular of all was his analysis of the difference between Spanish and English football, and the problem in this country with youth football.

Alex stated on MUTV:

"English teams are being handicapped by rules agreed between the Football Association and Premier League that prevent clubs working with youngsters aged 16 and under for any longer than 90 minutes a day. People have to understand the mechanics of the industry we are working in," Ferguson continued, "We are only allowed to coach youngsters for an hour and a half, they [Barcelona] can coach every hour of the day if they want to. That's the great advantage they have got. It is a fantastic philosophy. We hope that in years to come our coaches will be able to spend more time with young kids, to teach them the basics, the technical abilities and the confidence to keep the ball all the time. We are good at it, but not as good as Barcelona at this moment in time. It is a wonderful challenge and we should always accept a challenge."

Glen Hoddle, ex-England manager and now founder of the Glen Hoddle Academy (GHA) has a vision for the future. It was reported:

"The primary goal of the GHA will be to offer a genuine route back into professional football for some of the youngsters discarded by the professional system. Each year football clubs across Europe release hundreds of talented young players. Glenn is absolutely convinced that the decision on their future is made too early and that many, given a further year or two, would develop into valued professional players.

Hoddle believes that the way kids aged 6-10 are brought through is probably the most important period of time in their technical development and feels as a country we haven't done enough about it.

He feels the physical energy of the player is how they are judged and often many will simply miss the boat. He would like to see boys and girls having 1000's of touches on the ball in training rather than a kick here and there."

Can we all answer the questions and can our generation of coaches and administrators create a better playing field for our children?

The new directives can help us and I would genuinely feel that in time, they can change the mindset that is ingrained in many coaches, scouts, parents and players heads.

The Dutch philosophy is often highlighted as the way forward but this is only one model and other European countries have their own variations. The English FA have put together The Future Game programme modelled on the Europeans, with the Spanish methods leading the way.

The following is an example of youth football that I researched, country by country across Europe:

| Spain | France |
|---|---|
| 11 v 11 games not until Under 14s & Under 15s. | 11 v 11 games not until Under 13 & 14's. |
| Coaching – They play 5 a side on a smaller pitch or court to focus on passing and movement. The Spanish culture is possession football. | Coaching - work on technique with an emphasis on teaching the game and making the correct decisions on when to hold on to the ball. Skills refined later. |
| Success – 2010 World Champions, 2008 Euro Champions, 2011 Under 21 Euro Champions   Barcelona continue to   dominate the Champions League. | Success - 1998 World Cup Champions, 2000 Euro Champions. Have only qualified twice in the last 8 Under 21 tournaments. |
| **England** | **Germany** |
| 11 v 11 games at Under 11 (up to 2011) | 11 v 11 games not until Under 15 |
| Coaching - Gareth Southgate has called for a culture change on players' technical abilities rather than their physical stature. | Coaching - Germany has ten times more qualified coaches than in England. |
| Success - 1996 Euro semis, plus many failed World Cup attempts since 1966. | Success - more major semi-finals and finals than any other country. Current national team is being hailed as one of the finest young German teams ever. |
| **Holland** | **Italy** |
| 11 v 11 games not until Under 13 | 11 v 11 games not until Under 13 |
| Coaching - The Dutch are big believers in 4 v 4 with emphasis on drilling movement patterns into the players. They have a culture of playing 4-3-3 so a lot of focus is on team shape | Coaching- The Italians publish league tables at all age groups to develop a winning mentality with a focus on results. Defensive masters and very tactical. |
| Success - World Cup Finalists 2010. | Success - World Cup winners in 2006 and 3 times previous. |

The teams that routinely have deep, successful runs – Germany, Spain, Brazil and Argentina – don't get there by luck. They identify and develop talent with abilities.

They aren't genetically superior or have special DNA. For whatever reason, the vast resources of English football have been unable to crack the secret code. Southgate's plan's hold the right ingredients to propel forward.

Quoted in Henry Winter's piece in the Daily Telegraph, Southgate also made a cutting assessment of England's ability to find even the gems it does produce at youth level:

"I suppose we've had a Paul Scholes come through who would have been able to play in that Barcelona team because his quality of touch, pass appreciation, ability to play one-touch and to manipulate the ball was up there with them. But would we have produced lots of them like Xavi, Iniesta and Messi? I suspect not. We would probably have overlooked a lot of those and not necessarily at club level. It might have been years before that: at Sunday football level, the guy who was trying to win a league didn't pick the smaller kids."

Again, Southgate exposes the real nub of the issue here. Talented young footballers do not get the necessary opportunities to prove themselves because of a focus on athleticism and physicality that stems from the adults involved – coaches and parents – taking it all too seriously. The idea that kids' teams must win at all costs as young as the age of 10 or 11 is an overlooked but fundamental spanner in the development works of elite talent in English football, and it's heartening that Southgate recognises the problem.

Of course, playing like Barcelona is more a rhetorical weapon than a genuine aim, but do I hope that Southgate and the FA have a similar approach in mind, if not necessarily a copycat style of play. Some of football's most feted sides were and are the product of a system, innovation and institutional consistency. None of these are beyond the means of the English.

## Conclusions

Many will have read the guidelines issued to parents by the Football Association as part of their Respect campaign, which stress the same important points: positivity; support; not taking the game too seriously; focusing on skill rather than winning; maintaining confidence with helpful analysis; respect for officials. We can not change the history written in the many stories shared in this publication but we now have a chance of shaping the future together.

All young players make mistakes and parents try to help by screaming and shouting. Whilst writing this, I have just over heard a conversation where a guy bragged about the fact he used to run a school team. He claimed he was victorious in every game but he was "forever getting sent off". As if to say he was passionate and it was humorous. However, I imagine it was not humorous to the poor referee's, pushed to the point of having to send off an adult; nor the children trying to enjoy a game of football whilst these sending off offences where exhibited on the touchlines. In the same way that an ASBO should not be a badge-of-honour for a wayward youth; getting sent off is nothing for an adult to be proud of.

Being passionate is something I feel I am, though I chose to channel the passion into a positive energy, as many matchday managers, coaches and volunteers do every week, by helping and supporting our children in the game of football.

Looking deeper into this shows you the fine line between helping and hindering. All children are aware of a parent's presence and this creates some pressure, whatever the parent's perception of it all.

Children discern far more than we think and often infer things from the slightest word or gesture.

They do not always recognise a general expression of disappointment and believe it is directed at them. Head shaking, rolling of the eyes, looking away, kicking the ground – any of these can discourage children, and language intended to incite and encourage like "Get Rid!" and "Sort it Out" are as practically useless from the touchline as they are on the field of play.

There is a train of thought that many parents buy into, that children need to learn to live with this and that it will toughen them up to face bigger challenges, but the evidence refutes this. It is not about giving unqualified praise; this is wrong, especially when the child knows they have not played well. It is about being aware of all the above points and discussing performance at the right time, offering only constructive advice.

All in all we are only human and people will continue to not follow rules - such is life. . However, when you note the subtlety of the matters, you must wonder why a number of parents still openly threaten and abuse their own and others' children, genuinely believing that they are doing nothing wrong. It is astounding that these parents cannot see that their example may embarrass and subliminally condone similar behaviour from their child in the future.

Make no mistake; this sort of behaviour happens in most sports. The factual accounts of the behaviour of some impossibly expectant, middle-class tennis parents are the equal of anything coming from Hackney Marshes.

**"Parents can be part of the problem or part of the solution, and with those who receive caring and well-balanced support from their loved ones are more likely to overcome the challenge out there in football rather than those who choose to fulfill parental egos, hopes and dreams"**
Taken from the book Focused on Soccer by Bill Beswick.

Parental aggression was one of several factors that led the FA to introduce the Respect campaign. Whilst getting angry at kids football may seem silly, we should applaud the FA for recognising the problem and attempting to solve it. They and every other sport should not tolerate even a small degree of these dangerous and damaging actions.

You have read the evidence, and you have to concede that parental attitude and actions play at least an equal part in a child's sporting development as the coaching does. This being so, it is difficult to resist the proposition that we should invest as much money into educating parents on these issues as we do into formal coaching.

Clubs have enough to do, without having to educate parents, and with one fell swoop, I hope this book will give those out there trying to ignore the Respect campaign a kick up the what-not; and to those who already care, a chance to realise it's not just a problem at their club or locally but nationwide. The problem is simply not being tolerated any longer and now being stamped out.

I will conclude the conclusion (so to speak!), with two stories that will sum up the situation we find ourselves in. Both are real life experiences as are all the tales told along the way:

**Venue: Leeds United Centre of Excellence**
**Game: East Riding Girls Under 10s v Leeds United Under 10s**

I don't remember the score from this game, all I remember is the sound. A 7 a-side game in which two teams played and all you could hear was the stiff north easterly wind and the sound of the girl's voices, calling for the ball, or to mark the opposition. After being given instructions before the game by the coaches, both teams played with a freedom I'd never seen before. The game was well attended and only good play was applauded in a manner more fit for the opera. The sound of the ball was audible as it zipped across the surface. The girls played with confidence to try new things, without being berated by anybody. Will we ever see a day where this happens at every junior game…? I hope so.

**Venue: South Cave Playing Fields**
**Game: Burlington Jackdaws Under 9s v South Cave Under 9s**

Played a week after the infamous Rooney swearing on TV incident. Ryan Langham, an Under 9 for the Jackdaws was simply having the game of the season. Every blade of grass was covered on the South Cave pitch, as he played the centre forward position with such dedication and perseverance to win the ball back for his team. Ryan never liked playing in defence but to help his all round development, I used to play him there to learn how to defend - which he did so well. Ryan supports Liverpool, and at half time, I said to him "That performance out there at centre forward was outstanding. It was like Wayne Rooney himself".

Ryan looked disgruntled as I hadn't liked him to a Liverpool player, though a smile then appeared on his face… "Does that mean I can swear if I score a goal if I'm like Rooney?" Needless to say, I was pretty gob smacked, though this shows the influence on our young players of stars.

I'm sure there are other conclusions to be drawn from what I have discussed throughout the book. However, the best conclusion would be the belief that we can rid the beautiful game of the disease out there and maybe in ten years from now, look at when our 7 year olds have become 17 year olds, and 14 year olds become 24. As the new generation become the professional players, officials and coaches of the future, I hope that the lessons of the Respect campaign become the norm and its ethos is embedded into the psyche of our national game. A future shaped by the changes being implemented even as we speak.

## Solutions

Football can be a daunting challenge for many parents and carers, especially those that don't actively have an interest in the sport and yet they find their children enjoy the game in its many forms. Family communication through football can often be stifled by adults' lack of recognition that the children's game is not the adults' game. It is essential that adults contextualize football through childhood and feel confident trusting children to play their game in safe loosely supervised environments.

Intergenerational relationships can play a vital role in community cohesion and if children are allowed to form circles of trust both young and old generations can benefit in the long term.

Football can provide families with wonderful memories for life. There are many formats of the game which help children develop their social and technical skills. Family football is a fundamental introduction to a life long love of the game. Football in childhood should be focused on fun without expectations.

Football can be a passionate game and often ignites emotions that some of us find difficult to control. Children often mimic poor adult behaviour from the touchline where being angry, frustrated and negative can be considered the norm. This aspect of the game can be positively addressed at a very early age. Senior family members set the standard when playing and watching the game together at all levels. When football is played in the wider community, families often provide positive support and respect all participants which children instinctively respond to.

There is no real solution other than to demonstrate some of the theory discussed in this book and work as a club and a team. Most leagues have fair play awards and maybe a Respect award for teams respecting the campaign would be a good idea.

Many contributors on internet forums share their experiences on success and solutions. I've chosen the following from Leicester City to demonstrate how league clubs can actively get involved in supporting the campaign. It demonstrates the way the Respect campaign can work. Make your own mind up, and as I asked at the start: why did we need a campaign in the first place? Who is to blame? You decide! Enjoy your football, and keep safe. Together we can make this work. Thanks to all those who have helped in the writing of this book and **I look forward to a Second Edition with more positive stories than ever.**

The **FA RESPECT** Programme is still in its infancy and for those who watched Leicester City on March 5th 2011 as their Championship **RESPECT** Game fixture between **Leicester City FC vs Coventry City FC**, one can see the difference in how professional players are handling themselves when cautioned, accepting the referee's decision and walking away. This is all down to honouring decisions by those who are managing the game, and respect for one another.

Leicester City FC has shown its commitment to Grassroots Football and is one in only a handful of professional clubs who has been working with the local County FA to ensure those who play, manage, officiate or watch have an enjoyable experience being involved in the game.

The day of celebration started with the 2 captains and club officials meeting with the Match Officials to amongst the general pre-match talk was to highlight the importance of showing Respect. The Family Stand at Walkers Stadium was the focal point where County FA staff were giving out Respect goodies and balloons to children. The Sunday Football League, the latest Adult League to join the FA Respect Programme, received the FA Respect Certificate. Jason Aram, League Official to the League had a pitch side photo taken with other existing Respect Leagues prior to the RESPECT flag leading the teams on the pitch.

## Update March 2011 sent to me by Dermot Collins

Since the launch of Respect F.C. on January 17, 17,000 supporters have joined the club and the Chairman's message delivered by Mark Watson with the assistance of Steve Claridge, Neil Ruddock and Chris Kamara has attracted 110,000 viewings. The resulting coverage was featured on BBC Breakfast News, NewsRound, Soccer AM, Football Focus, ITV's transmission of the FA Cup 5th Rd draw, Radio Five Live, Talk Sport, 10 of the BBC Regional Radio stations and a feature article on the UEFA website. Respect F.C. was also promoted at the FA Cup 4th round ties with many clubs actively promoting Respect F.C. in their staging of ties.

The Respect F.C. website provides an opportunity for supporters to contribute to Respect-related discussions. Over 800 comments have been received to date with the general themes being;

1. Support for Respect to deal with behavioural problems in football
2. The poor example set by professional players
3. The failure of referees to deal with the poor behaviour of professional players
4. The poor standard of refereeing that leads to dissent and disrespect

Of these themes by far the commonest were 2 & 3.

## Disciplinary Statistics

These statistics are only of real value at the end of the season and may have been distorted slightly by postponements arising from bad weather but as of 1 March the collated disciplinary statistics indicate that:

- The volume of dissent cautions are down in 10 out of 16 of the senior leagues. Overall across the top four divisions dissent cautions are down by 19%. .

FA Misconduct Charges in the Professional Game 2010/11 as of February 3rd (comparative 2010/11 figures are in brackets)

- Surrounding a Match Official – 1(1)  charge,
                                    3 (0) warnings/reminders
- Mass Confrontation  -  17 (25) charges,  28 (20) warnings/reminders
- Technical Area  Offences - 21 (19), charges
                                    13 (19) warnings/reminders

## Referee recruitment

As of 15 January 2011 male referees (levels 1-8)  were up to 26,889 an increase of 5% from 2010 and up by over 5,000 from the 21,876 base level in the 2008 National Game Strategy. Overall female referees (levels 1-8) were up to 853, an increase of 12.1% from 2010.

## Referee satisfaction

Each week match officials involved in games which are entered onto the FA's Full Time management system are encouraged to submit "Respect marks". This season 3900 referees have entered marks for over 15,000

games. The results for this are as follows (variance from last year in brackets):
National Averages (out of 5):

- Coach Manager Behaviour = 4.2 (+0.1)
- Player Behaviour = 4.0 (no change)
- Spectator Behaviour = 4.2 (+0.1)
- Effectiveness of the captains in taking responsibility for their team's behaviour = 3.8 (no change)
- Overall behaviour at this Match = 4.0 (no change)
- Match Official enjoyment = 4.1 (no change )

Overall this indicates that although there is room for improvement most match officials have an enjoyable experience of officiating and are treated with respect by most participants.

**Respect On Line Training for Referees**

An online Respect course has been developed which illustrates the practical assistance the Respect measures can offer to referees. The course includes tips and guidance from some of the country's top referees as well as realistic match scenarios and can be found on the Respect pages of the FA.com

**Other Indicators**
To improve the education of Coaches and Parents as to how they can better support young players we have devised an on Line Respect course for coaches and parents. This course is now an obligatory part of the FA's Level One Coaching Award and has now been completed by over 25,000 users since its launch.

Of the FA's 1150 affiliated leagues, 850 are now confirmed as Respect Leagues. Those that remain outside the programme largely do so because they believe they have superior programmes in place or, as volunteers, feel unable to take on additional initiatives.

## Other Activity

### Respect and Citizenship Resource

A resource has been developed for use in education which links the Respect programmes with wider discussions on Citizenship and sporting ethics. It has been circulated free of charge to all schools, colleges, academies, centres of excellence and Chartered Standard community clubs. The initial reaction has been very positive.

### Respect Awards

The 2011 Respect Awards were launched on 19 January. There are 13 categories of award spanning the game with the winners of the Respect Awards and Fair Play Awards picking up their awards and cash prize at an end of season FA match. It should be noted that the individual award is also open to nominations for referees that do an outstanding job in promoting and upholding Respect. The closing date for nominations is 1 April.

**Respect on the FA.com** – The Respect pages on the FA.com have been revised and improved and provide a far clearer means of downloading resources.

**Respect for Small Sided Football** – The roll out of this scheme continues to be delayed until the disciplinary process for Small Sided Football has been agreed. It is hoped that a Forum in February will resolve these difficulties and allow for roll out soon after.

## Taken from a visiting team to our club in 2011

The team I coached played a league match one evening in Bridlington. Prior to kick off, the referee approached me and explained what he expected from me, the players in my team and the coaches of both teams. I advised the ref that he would not have a problem with me as the coach nor the players/parents etc. After the match finished, which we drew, the ref came over for a chat. The referee praised my lads on their level of sportsmanship during and after the match, as well as the coaching team, parents etc...it proves that working with the Respect campaign is better than working against it...it can work!

The game was fantastic and finished 1-1. I sent a text to the opposition club the next day to congratulate them on the excellent environment they had in structure at their club.

## And finally...

Gary Lineker put together a TV programme on the burning issue in 2010. This piece in the Daily Mail led me to the publishing of this book. I hope Lineker and Southgate both read it...I can hope.

"Anti-social behaviour is going to be one of the issues at this General Election. But it isn't just limited to town centres on a Saturday night. I have stood on the touchline for many years, watching my four boys, George, Harry, Tobias and Angus, play football. And if you'd seen some of the behaviour from parents that I've witnessed, you'd be completely shocked.

Swearing at the referee, abusing the manager or shouting at their own kids - it is not a pretty sight. It's got so bad at times that I've felt it necessary to have a quiet word with some of them to tone it down, politely suggesting that their 'commitment' isn't actually helping their own sons relax and enjoy playing the game.

If I was Prime Minister for a day, I'd introduce a blanket rule that many Premier League academies already have in place - that parents on the touchline can only applaud, not criticise. When my third son, Tobias, joined the Chelsea Academy, I and other parents attended a meeting that spelled out how we had to behave if we wanted to be spectators. It was confirmed later in a letter.

I think it's a great idea and should be introduced for all schools matches and junior football on a Sunday morning. It reminded me of when I went to Ajax to make a television documentary about their famed youth system. I remember the applause from watching parents when something good happened on the pitch - and patient silence if a pass went astray or a referee made a big decision.

It was a very healthy experience, in my view. Let me make it clear, the overwhelming number of parents who watch their children play football are well-behaved and proud of their kids, however good they are.

The managers, coaches and referees give up their time for free and so if they're not perfect or make the odd mistake, so what? They are doing a lot more good than bad. But there is a breed of parent I've seen who hurl ridiculous abuse at the officials or even the young player they are meant to be supporting.

It is as if they are living their own dreams through their kids. They put far too much pressure on them and the results can be shocking - and, in the long term, no good for the overall standard of our football.

Last season, I went to a tournament where one of my boys was playing and another dad bellowed furiously at his son throughout the game - 99 per cent of it rubbish like 'Kick it out', 'Don't get caught' or 'Don't dribble with it there'.

One of the advantages of being known as a former player was I felt confident enough to have a discreet word with this man and suggest his comments weren't helping his boy perform. His attitude is one of the reasons we haven't produced as many footballers as we should have done over the years.

In Spain, the fans don't like to see players boot the ball into touch. But here, from eight or nine, there is some mortal fear about losing possession, which is why it's ingrained at such a young age to play the percentage pass. Starting young: Enjoyment is the most important part of the game

Personally, I tried to encourage my kids to try a trick or attempt a dribble, and they would always worry about the repercussions from team-mates or the other spectators about losing the ball. Kids that age shouldn't be frightened in that way. It is about enjoying the sport above anything else.

The parents who shout inane and critical comments are bad enough, but I've also seen them turn on the team coach, who is probably giving up his time for free. I never understood that. The parent wouldn't storm into the middle of a math's lesson and shout in front of all the children: 'You are teaching them to add up wrong.' So why do it at a football game?

I've seen referees walk off because of the abuse they get from parents and, in the worst case I can remember, a young lad - a talented player, as it happens - was physically dragged off by his dad, who was so disappointed in his performance. I'd heard the dad shout at the lad after he'd missed a chance and, sure enough, his confidence drained even further after that. I didn't see the father strike the boy, but it was as close as you could get - it was menacing because he'd let the passion in wanting to see his son do well boil over into desperation.

They can't even control their own behaviour, so how they think they can begin to control their children, I don't know.

I know sport cannot be the major issue in a General Election, with the economic downturn and a war in Afghanistan, not to mention the future of our hospitals and schools. But I still think it is an undervalued issue.

Sport helps to keep our population healthy, particularly children, and encourages discipline, teamwork and other qualities that help you in life generally. Why should a minority of mouthy parents ruin things?

There seems to be a problem in our society generally about teenagers going off the rails and you suspect there might be a lack of care or love in the household where they grew up.

I'm not a politician or social worker, but in the field I do know - football - it's time for the pushy parents to leave their kids alone. They would be much better off giving encouragement. And if they can't do that, it's best for them to say nothing at all."

# Sources

Thank you to the following people who gave me permission to quote from their websites or other literature produced. I have made every attempt to credit these sources when used:

Dermot Collins – FA Respect Manager
Paul Cooper - Give Us Back Our Game
Ernie Brennan - National Children's Football Alliance
Colin Dowdy - Sale United
Mal Lee – Don't X The Line

I have also read countless newspaper articles, websites and internet forums. I have tried to credit accurately wherever possible but please get in touch if you feel there has been an oversight.

# Thanks

First of all a thanks to parents involved with the Burlington jackdaws Respect Campaign 2010-11

Players: Lachlon Chadwick, Cameron Smith, Conor Benson, Corey Reen, Finn Tudor, Louis Hart, Louie Leadley, Marc Surtis, Oliver Carr, Jacob Lawer, Jack O Shea, Jay Smith, Elliot Day, Decan Mooney, Cameron Connelly, Ryan Galloway, Frankie Gascoigne, Jack Sumner, Jacob O' Brien, Jed Oyston, Louis Beckett, Dan Mellonby, Jack Gavin, Mani Goacher, Brandon Colley, Jacob James, Josh Brown, Josh Stanyon, Thomas Stanyon, Miller Thomas-Haynes, Rhys Kelly, Ryan Langham, Lily Mae Andrew, Harry Johnston, Llyod Brodie, Louie Miller, Ashley Melles, Lewis Grainger, Harry Boreman, Taylor Barber, Thomas McEwan, Rhys Sedgewck, Robert Dean Sam Goacher, Harry Ellis, Ben Coates, Oliver Brown, Jordan Booth, Lewis Lamb, Connor Mckinary, Elliott Brown, Oliver Beckett, Ryan Petre, Jack Panhaussen, Joel Ellis Beesting, Jordan Ball, Zach Hunter

Coaches: Adam Yhklef, Billy Tyler, Paul Webb, Nick Tudor, Joel Rollinson, Chris Jenkinson, Criddy Brown, Marcus Gascoigne, Mike Grainger and after school coach Frank Belt and Bridlington Sports Club 1st team and Globe Old Boys team.

Thanks go to the contributors within this book:

Stewart Smith, Paul Cooper, Mal Lee, Dermot Collins, Lesley Allon, Helen Hever, Graham Taylor, Bobby Charlton Soccer Schools, Andy Ripley, Barry Scott, David Bailey, Mike English, Elain Fillingham, Steven Taylor and Jay Cochrane. Along with all the coaches I have had the pleasure to work with over the years, from recently in Bagpuss, to my good pal Paddy to the experienced Bryn Cooper (the bloke that found Ryan Giggs )

Thanks to the sources which I have used:

The BBC, Football 365, footy4kids, Sky Sports, Talksport, The Daily Mail, The Sun, The Telegraph, The Mirror

And Finally:

Thanks to all those who have supported me during my coaching years and through the writing of this book.

This book was produced as part of the People's History of Football Series. For further information about the series, or if you are interested in writing a football book, visit:

www.peopleshistoryoffootball.com

or email: info@peopleshistoryoffootball.co.uk